HM
SUBMARINES
IN CAMERA

HM SUBMARINES IN CAMERA

1901-1996

COMMANDER J.J. TALL AND PAUL KEMP

FOREWORD BY

REAR ADMIRAL J. F. PEROWNE OBE

FLAG OFFICER SUBMARINES

SUTTON PUBLISHING

First published in 1996 by
Sutton Publishing Limited · Phoenix Mill
Thrupp · Stroud · Gloucestershire · GL5 2BU

British Library Cataloguing in Publication Data
A catalogue record for this book is available from the British Library

ISBN 0-7509-0875-0

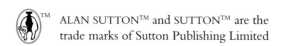

ALAN SUTTON™ and SUTTON™ are the
trade marks of Sutton Publishing Limited

Typeset in 11/15 pt Baskerville.
Typesetting and origination by
Sutton Publishing Limited.
Printed in Great Britain by
Butler & Tanner, Frome, Somerset.

CONTENTS

FOREWORD

I am delighted to be associated with *HM Submarines in Camera* for two reasons. Firstly as Flag Officer Submarines and thus the current head of the Submarine branch of the Royal Navy, and secondly as the son of a Second World War submarine officer who went on to command his own boats. I am therefore highly conscious of what it takes to be a submariner in any era, and the photographs in this book show the enormous changes in submarine development made since 1901. The images, though, show much more than technology – they bring into focus the conditions under which men served, and explain why submariners as a breed are at the same time intensely loyal to one another, fiercely proud of the achievements of their service, and highly conscious of the sacrifice of those who died in both war and peace in defence of their country. Any leg-pulling by my father about comfort when he visited me in my SSN HMS *Superb* was soon tempered by his obvious pride in both man and machine which represented the legacy gifted by his generation to the modern submarine force.

If this book stimulates your interest in submarine history, then I strongly commend to you a visit to HMS *Alliance* and the Royal Navy Submarine Museum in Gosport, because there you will find the soul of our Submarine Service. As well as tracing the history of the submarine throughout the ages, and displaying hundreds of items of personal memorabilia of those who served in submarines, the museum is a living tribute to more than 5,000 of our forebears who were killed in action and whose names are recorded in the Book of Remembrance.

Despite the reduction in size of the Royal Navy, the Submarine Service stands, and will continue to stand, at the forefront of the defence of the UK. After the warming-up of the Cold War, it was inevitable that changes in strategy in underwater warfare had to be made. However with the recent introduction of the 'Vanguard' class SSBN the Submarine Service now provides the sole national nuclear deterrent in both the strategic and sub-strategic roles through its Trident missiles. Our present and future SSNs will continue to police the seas worldwide, and will become increasingly integrated with our surface Fleet, bringing with them a new land attack role with their Tomahawk missiles. I know that historians among you will be aware that such an integration was attempted just after the First World War with the ill-fated steam driven 'K' and 'M' classes, however, having learnt the lessons of past failures, I am determined that we shall succeed this time. Thus the modern Submarine Service can look forward with confidence to its future. Through *HM Submarines in Camera* it can also look back with enormous pride on a great tradition established in a remarkably short period of time.

Rear Admiral
J.F. Perowne OBE,
Flag Officer Submarines

INTRODUCTION

This book is an attempt to illustrate something of the history of the Royal Navy's Submarine Service in the ninety-three years since HM Submarine No. 1 was commissioned. Although the majority of the photographs in this book are of the submarines which have worn the White Ensign since 1903, we have also tried to capture a little of the flavour of submarine life throughout this period. We have compiled a representative selection of photographs to show the boats, the personalities of the Submarine Service and the conditions in which they served. In those ninety-three years since Submarine No. 1 put to sea under the White Ensign, the submarine has undergone tremendous change. No. 1 was small, unhealthy (if not downright dangerous) to live in and its ability unproven. The nuclear-powered submarines in today's Royal Navy have changed unbelievably since those early days. Nothing illustrates that change better than the photographs in this book. Inevitably there are areas of submarine history which, for reasons of space, we have had to omit. These include submarine bases and depot ships, although the often unacknowledged contribution to the history of the Submarine Service made by the staff of these organizations should not be forgotten.

The emphasis placed on technological change and development tends to hide the one factor in submarine history which is constant – the human element: the commanding officer and the submarine's crew. Technology may have changed out of all recognition but if Petty Officer William Waller, the first submarine coxswain, were to report on board HMS *Vanguard*, there would be much that he would find familiar.

Only the submarine's commanding officer and crew can ensure success and it is on their skill, courage, endurance and determination that the ultimate verdict rests. The Royal Navy has been more than fortunate in the quality of the officers and men who have served in submarines. They have in a very short period created a tradition which will stand the test of time.

This book is offered as a tribute to more than 5,000 officers and men of the Royal Navy's Submarine Service who have lost their lives in peace and war. All royalties from this book are being donated to the Submarine Memorial Benevolent Fund.

J.J. Tall & Paul Kemp
Gosport, June 1996

ACKNOWLEDGEMENTS

The authors are deeply grateful to the following for their help in the preparation of this book: Gus Britton, Brian Head, David Hill, Peter Jung, Bernd Langensiepen, Keith Lintott, Achille Rastelli and David Webb. Special thanks are due to those members of the staff of the Royal Navy Submarine Museum who have given tremendous support for the book: Margaret Bidmead, Debbie Corner and Julie Nesbit. This project was begun by Commander Richard Compton-Hall, former Director of the Submarine Museum, and was taken over on his retirement. We hope that he is pleased with the final product. The authors are particularly grateful to Rear Admiral J.F. Perowne for contributing the foreword.

Unless otherwise stated, all photographs in the book are from the Archives of the Royal Navy Submarine Museum. Copies of these photographs can be obtained by writing to the Keeper of the Photographs. The authors are grateful to the National Maritime Museum, Museo Storico Navale in Venice, *Navy News*, Wright & Logan and Vickers for permission to use the photographs in their collections. Crown Copyright photographs are reproduced by permission of the Controller of Her Majesty's Stationery Office. The authors have tried to trace the copyright holders of all the photographs used in this book. In certain cases it has not been possible to trace the copyright holder. The authors apologise if any copyright has been accidentally infringed.

THE FIRST
SUBMERSIBLES

Today the Submarine Service has a central role in the defence of this country. With the Trident D5 ballistic missile, the Service maintains and operates a weapon of unimaginable destructive power, while the thirteen fleet submarines of the 'Swiftsure' and 'Trafalgar' classes are the most potent individual units in the Royal Navy's order of battle.

Ninety-five years ago, in 1901, the position of the submarine was anything but central in the Royal Navy. Ever since the end of the Napoleonic Wars in 1815, Britain had maintained a *Pax Britannica* through her possession of a battle fleet that was larger than that of any other power. Although the Admiralty had taken notice of the development of submarines in other countries, notably France and the United States, British policy was to steer clear of this new addition to the naval armoury. The submarine was seen as the weapon of the weaker power and its success threatened Britain's traditional command of the seas. Viscount Goschen, first Lord of

the Admiralty, expressed the position admirably in a statement to the House of Commons in April 1900: 'The Admiralty are not prepared to take any steps with regard to the submarines because this vessel is only the weapon of the weaker nation.'

A year later the position had been reversed and in April 1901, Viscount Selbourne announced that five submarine vessels would be purchased, 'to assist the Admiralty in assessing their true value'. Since no British design was available, the naval attaché in Washington was quickly despatched to purchase the rights to designs by the American inventor John Holland. The construction work was carried out by Vickers.

From little acorns oak trees grow and this was the case with the infant Submarine Service. The first five 'Holland' boats were followed by the 'A' class – the first all-British design. The 'B', 'C', 'D' and 'E' classes then followed, each representing a step forward in size, armament, propulsion and habitability. The 'E' class is particularly worthy of note. It was an unspectacular but solid design that served throughout the First World War in all theatres of operations and proved capable of absorbing the numerous modifications made as a result of this war experience.

At the same time as the submarines were developing, their crews were gaining knowledge and experience of the new crafts. Regarded with a certain amount of superiority by their colleagues in the surface fleet (serving in submarines was 'no occupation of a gentleman'), the early submariners relished the responsibility, self-discipline and the challenges offered by this new arm of the Service. The officers were all relatively junior, Lieutenant Commanders or below, and therefore had no body of experience to fall back on, but in contrast, the ratings were all men of long service and good conduct. In pre-war exercises the submarine proved that it could operate against surface ships with success, although these early achievements were used to make claims for future performance which could not, in the end, be delivered.

The submarines of the 'C', 'D' and 'E' classes bore the brunt of naval operations during the First World War. Although there were newer submarines available in 1914, the fruits of the 1912 Submarine Design Committee, the design process which had begun with the 'A' class and culminated with the 'E' class had been interrupted and it was not until the introduction of the 'L' class in 1917 that submarine construction was back on course.

In home waters British submarines operated in the North Sea as part of the general blockade of the High Seas Fleet but as the German anti-submarine campaign progressed, they found themselves engaged in anti-submarine patrols in the northern area of the North Sea and in the Western Approaches. Although some significant successes against German capital ships were scored, on the whole these patrols were conducted against a background of bad weather; only a good deal of hard work by their crews, supported by the staff of the depot ships, kept the boats running. British submarines were the first units of the fleet to go 'in harms way' during 1914 and were the last to return to port in 1918.

It was in the Baltic and the Mediterranean that British submariners found glory. In the Baltic, 'E' class submarines which had made the hazardous passage through the Skaggerak and Kattegat, disrupted the vital iron-ore trade between Germany and Sweden. So successful were their operations that the Germans re-named the Baltic the 'Hortonsee' after Lieutenant Max Horton, commanding officer of *E.9*. The submariners endured the rigours of the Russian winters and only ceased operations when Russia withdrew from the war following the revolution.

In the Mediterranean, British submarines made the hazardous passage through the nets and minefields of the Dardanelles to operate in the Sea of Marmara. They were working against Turkish shipping supplying their troops on the Gallipoli peninsula. Although their operations did not materially affect the campaign, they were of incalculable value for morale and confirmed that the submarine had real potential as a weapon. Four of the five VCs awarded to British submariners during the First World War were for operations in this theatre. Among those decorated were: Lieutenant N.D. Holbrook of *B.11*, Commander E.C. Boyle of *E.14*, Lieutenant Commander M. Nasmith of *E.11* and Lieutenant Commander G.S. White of *E.14*. The price of this success was high; 56 submarines did not return from patrol and 1,174 officers and men were killed. Commodore Sydney Hall, head of the Submarine Service, was more than justified in his praise when he wrote: 'Your steadfastness and your grit, while the toll of your gallant fellows was heavy, have been beyond all praise and will form glorious pages in our naval history when this comes to be written.'

The beginning. HM Submarine Torpedo Boat No. 1 (more generally known as 'Holland 1') entered the water at Barrow on 2 October 1901. She was the first of five boats built by Vickers under licence from the Holland Torpedo Boat Co. Although the first to be launched, No. 1 did not enter service until 2 February 1903 by which time all her sisters were in service. The five 'Hollands' were built to a 'spindle-hull' design: a circular profile around a central axis with all tanks and machinery contained within the pressure hull. Conditions inside the craft were thus appallingly cramped for the crew of two officers and six ratings.

Captain Reginald Bacon RN, the first Inspecting Captain of Submarines and head of the embryonic Submarine Service. Bacon was one of the most technically minded officers of his day but his complete intolerance of anyone whose views failed to match his own made him difficult to work with. Bacon went on to greater things: he was the first commanding officer of HMS *Dreadnought*, and after retiring to take up a position in the armaments industry he returned to active service in 1914 to command the Dover Patrol.

Holland 2 under way with the Captain Bacon standing on the left. A lieutenant is steering the boat as there are no ratings 'up top'. The periscope can be seen behind the open hatch, complete with its bracing wire. The other three vertical tubes are ventilators which were required to vent the boat and battery as well as providing additional fresh air for the engine. This photograph shows the very low freeboard of the 'Holland' which restricted operations to coastal waters and then only in calm conditions.

Petty Officer William Waller, the first submarine coxswain in the Royal Navy. On his left arm are crossed anchors and crown indicating his rate as a petty officer, with three stripes indicating more than twelve years' long service and good conduct. On his right arm is the crossed torpedoes and wheel badge of a Torpedo Coxswain. Waller's duties included steering the craft – both on the surface and submerged – and being responsible for the discipline of the ratings in the ship's company. This latter task was hardly onerous as the other five ratings would be men of long service like himself.

Holland 2 alongside the depot ship HMS *Hazard*. The rating on the right is sitting on the binnacle, which housed the magnetic compass as it could not be kept within the all-steel hull of the submarine. When the submarine was dived, the compass was viewed via a small periscope with the compass card illuminated by an electric bulb. At the top of the short mast are the two oil lamps used when the submarine was running on the surface at night.

Holland 1, trimmed down and ready to commence a static dive. The diving procedure was very slow; it took anything from 2 to 10 minutes to take a 'Holland' boat from the surface to periscope depth. The periscope is shown raised and braced; it had to be braced since it lacked sufficient strength to stand unsupported. The main problem with using the periscope was that when looking forward, the object in view was seen upright; when looking on the beam the object was seen on its side and when looking astern the object was seen inverted. This caused considerable confusion, not to mention a certain amount of hilarity, during exercises and torpedo practice.

Holland 5 aground at 'Promotion Point' off Fort Blockhouse on 24 August 1910. The grounding was the result of navigational error but the highly public location of the incident – in full view of the Inspecting Captain of Submarines – meant that the commanding officer's reputation was bound to suffer. Hence the name 'Promotion Point'. The photograph gives a good view of the *Holland*'s hull form. The spindle-hull form was not ideal, however. It had poor longitudinal stability and a low reserve of buoyancy, and was liable to plunge in a swell.

The low reserve of buoyancy of the Hollands is shown well in this photograph of *Holland 4* on the surface, with Lieutenant J. Inglis by the hatch. The freeboard in the 'Holland' was so low (only four feet from hatch to waterline in the light condition) that the hatch had to be kept closed in any sea other than a flat calm. In rough weather the watchkeeper's position on the exposed casing was almost untenable. The solution was to raise the (upper) hatch by constructing a conning tower. *Holland 2* was given such a feature in 1905 and was the only one of the class to be thus fitted.

Lieutenant Max Horton with the crew of *Holland 3* in January 1906. A feature to note in this photograph is that none of the ratings has less than eight years' service, as is indicated by their good conduct stripes – one stripe awarded for every four years' service. Horton is the most distinguished submariner in the Royal Navy's history. During the First World War he was the first submarine commander to sink an enemy warship (the German cruiser *Hela* on 13 September 1914), and he then commanded the submarine *E.9* in the Baltic with considerable distinction before returning to command the submarines *J.1* and *M.1*. His career then followed the classic pattern of command at sea interspersed with staff appointments ashore. On the outbreak of the Second World War, Horton was a Vice Admiral and, following a three-year appointment as head of the Submarine Service, he was appointed Commander in Chief Western Approaches in November 1942 and oversaw the defeat of the U-boats in the Battle of the Atlantic.

HM Submarine *A.1*, first of the thirteen boats of the 'A' class. The 'A' class was a larger version of the 'Holland', but built to an all-British design following the end of Vickers' relationship with the Holland Torpedo Boat Co. The raised conning tower was fitted to all boats in the class and was a standard feature of submarine construction thereafter. As an additional safety feature the conning tower had two hatches: the upper hatch which led out onto the bridge and the lower hatch which

sealed off the conning tower from the control room. Reports from sea indicated that the 'A' class represented a considerable improvement on the 'Holland'. *A.1*'s commanding officer, Lieutenant Mansergh, reported that: 'She behaved well and could keep an even depth at quite moderate speed whereas the earlier boats had to be trimmed fine and kept at full speed while working submerged.'

A group of ratings on *A.1*'s conning tower. The cap tallies bear the name of HMS *Mercury*, the depot ship to which *A.1* was attached. The rating in the foreground is holding a 'tea-urn'. Although the early submarine service was usually characterized as being 'dirty', this photograph shows that the crew have taken some care over the appearance of their boat. The ventilators are highly polished, the heaving lines are neatly coiled down on the deck and all ferrous metal is freshly painted.

Chief ERA Charles Sinden who was killed in an explosion onboard *A.5* at Queenstown on 16 February 1905. The explosion was a result of a build-up of petrol fumes inside the boat resulting from a badly packed gland in the petrol pump. When the order to start the engine to ventilate the boat was given, the fumes exploded. Four other members of *A.5*'s crew died in the explosion.

A.7 fitted with experimental hydroplanes on her conning tower. The boats of the 'Holland' and 'A' classes were fitted with one set of 'diving rudders' aft, as the operation of diving the boat was performed while she was stationary. As early submariners grew more experienced, they found that they could dive their craft while under way and that another set of 'diving rudders' was necessary. Conning tower hydroplanes were not a standard fitting in the 'A' class boats.

A.12 trimmed down by stern so that the bow caps and torpedo tubes can be inspected. In order to ensure the submarine's stability during this operation, it would be lifted by means of a block and tackle secured to one of the depot ship's davits. The original caption for this photograph reads, 'Are you sure it's not loaded?'

A.13 at sea and en route to Portsmouth from Barrow in 1907. *A.13*, the last of the A-boats, was the first British submarine to be fitted with a diesel engine. The engine was a Hornsby-Ackroyd six-cylinder of 500 b.h.p. The diesel was heavier than the petrol engine fitted in other boats of the class and consequently fuel stowage was reduced. Nevertheless, on passage from Barrow to Portsmouth, the engine ran for 29½ hours – an extremely good performance for the time.

B.1 on completion at Barrow in 1905. The eleven boats of the 'B' class represented a 50 per cent increase in size on the 'A' class with consequent improvements in endurance. There was, however, no improvement in conditions for the crew of two officers and thirteen ratings. The crew slept where they could on the deck. Little fresh food was carried – it was assumed that the submarines would be operational in coastal waters and never far from port – and what hot food could be prepared was heated on a hotplate. There were no heads and the crew simply relieved themselves over the side or, when the boat was dived, used a bucket which was then emptied over the side when the boat surfaced. The photograph shows *B.1* with a modified bow form achieved by building a casing over the pressure hull. This improved stability, made working on the upper deck easier for the crew and provided a housing for such items of equipment as capstans and cable holders.

Lieutenant Basil Beal on the fore casing of *B.1* in 1914 wearing typical foul weather clothing of the period. A 'Lammy' or 'Duffle' coat is worn over the uniform jacket, together with leather gauntlets and heavy sea boots. The boots were usually worn a size larger than needed. If the wearer fell overboard the boots could fill with water and take the wearer down. A larger size allowed for easier removal. Beal, one of the earliest officers to specialize in submarines, was killed in March 1917 when in command of *E.49*.

Although the 'B' class had been replaced by newer and more potent submarines by the outbreak of the First World War, it was *B.11* under the command of Lieutenant Norman Holbrook that caught the nation's imagination by sinking the Turkish coast defence battleship *Messudieh* in the Dardanelles on 13 December 1914. Holbrook and his ship's company are shown after the attack on the depot ship HMS *Blenheim*. Holbrook (rear row centre with folded arms) was awarded the Victoria Cross, the first naval VC of the First World War and the first of 14 submariners to win this, the highest British gallantry award. Holbrook's first lieutenant, Lieutenant Sydney Winn, was awarded the DSO and every other man in the crew was awarded the DSM. The scale of awards to *B.11*'s crew was unusual and was never repeated for other submarine crews.

B.1, 3, 4 and *5* spent the First World War in home waters. The remainder went to the Mediterranean and served in the Adriatic based at Venice, where they arrived in November 1915. This photograph shows *B.8, 6, 11* and *10* secured at Arsenal in Venice in 1916. Their role was to assist the Italians in patrols off the main Austrian Naval base at Pola (now Pula). The British senior submarine officer at Venice, Commander Wilfrid Tomkinson, none too pleased at being sent to Venice from commanding a destroyer in the Harwich Force, was consoled by Commodore Hall with the words, 'you are nearer to Pola than we are to Kiel'.

Museo Storico Navale, Venice

B.6 on the surface and trimmed down while on patrol off Pola. Submarine tactics at this time were largely a matter of experiment and, with the primitive nature of the equipment available at the time, it was considered that to spend the day dived, even when near to an enemy base, might not be particularly productive. Accordingly, submariners compromised, trimming the boat down so that only the conning tower remained above the surface. However, in the Adriatic where the water (on the Austrian side) was clear and where Austrian air patrols were frequent and vigilant, this practice proved near-fatal on two occasions: both *B.9* on 30 March and *B.7* on 4 June 1916 endured a rough time at the hands of Austrian aircraft.

B.10 up in dry dock after being bombed and sunk in an Austrian air raid on 9/10 August 1910. *B.10* was the first submarine to be sunk by air attack although, if the truth be told, her sinking was an additional bonus for the Austrian airmen who simply dropped their bombs indiscriminately over the Arsenal and headed for home. The first submarine to be sunk by a deliberate air attack was the French *Fouccault*, also sunk by Austrian aircraft on 15 September 1916. B.10 was docked for repairs but the air raid damage was compounded by the activities of an Italian dockyard welder who began work with his torch next to one of the submarine's petrol tanks which was full at the time. The only way that the resulting fire could be quenched was by flooding the dock. *B.10* was surveyed and considered not fit for repair. She was sold locally for breaking up.

Museo Storico Navale, Venice

HMS *C.1* in a floating dock. The thirty-eight 'C' class submarines represented an increase in size on the 'B' class but otherwise little changed. The craft were still of the spindle-hull form, armed with two 18 inch torpedoes, and powered by a petrol engine and still possessed of the unwholesome living conditions. In this photograph the bow cap and inner door for the starboard torpedo tube are visible. A new feature of submarine design was the introduction of two periscopes, one for the commanding officer and the other for continuous use by the lookout.

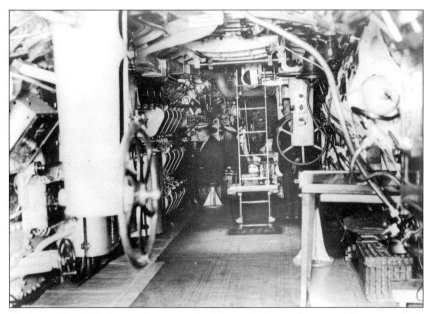

An internal view of a 'C' class submarine looking aft from the control room. As in the three previous classes of submarine, there were no internal bulkheads. The helmsman is standing behind the wheel on the right looking into the small periscope which enabled him to view the magnetic compass mounted on the hull. The ladder in the centre leads up to the bridge and to the left of it are the main and auxiliary switches for the electric motors. Behind the helmsman is the main engine. The table on the right is the wardroom table and underneath it is a hamper probably containing the officers' food!

The two petrol engines in a 'C' class submarine's engine room looking aft. The crankcase cover between the two engines acted as a walkway through to the main motors and clutches. The heads consisted of a bucket which was kept aft of the engines. Anybody using this facility had to perform in full view of the engine or motor watchkeepers.

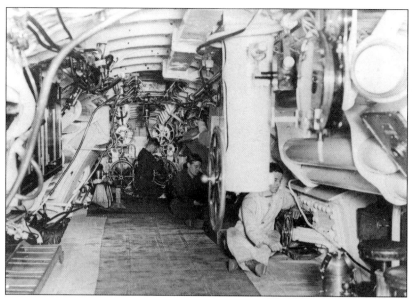

Looking forward in a 'C' class submarine toward the two 18 inch torpedo tubes. The two ratings seated on the right are operating the Kingston valves. The wheel in the centre is for the forward hydroplanes and to the right of this can be seen two of the high pressure air cylinders used for blowing the ballast tanks and turning the main engines. The word which best describes submarine life is 'squalid'. There was limited headroom so that anyone of above average height would find life extremely uncomfortable. The lack of internal bulkheads meant that there was no privacy. Officers and men slept anywhere on the canvas-covered deck where they could find a space. Little food was carried and cooking facilities were rudimentary and consisted of little more than a hotplate. Yet there was never a shortage of volunteers for service in submarines.

C.11 in the floating dock in Haslar Creek with her commanding officer, Lieutenant C.G. Brodie RN, standing on the hull, aft of the conning tower. Brodie was one of only three survivors from this submarine when she was sunk off Cromer on 14 July 1909 following a collision with the merchant ship *Eddystone*.

A unique photograph showing *C.3* embarking fuel from petrol lighter No. 34. The petrol was shipped in barrels and then transferred into the submarine by hand pump. It was common practice to have a spare crew available when taking on petrol, as the fumes in the submarine's small and cramped interior caused symptoms akin to drunkenness among the crew. Sailors thus afflicted had to be taken out into the fresh air to recover.

C.38 arriving at Hong Kong on 20 April 1911 after a remarkable 72-day journey with *C.36* and *C.37*. The ships were towed part of the way but mostly used their own engines, although they did not dive while on passage. The voyage was a considerable achievement and did much to convince those in authority with reservations about the potential of submarines, that these craft were capable of more than defensive operations. These three boats remained at Hong Kong until 1919 when they were sold for scrap.

C.14 in dry dock after being salvaged following her collision with Government Hopper No. 29 on 10 December 1913 in Plymouth Sound. This was the seventh occasion on which a British submarine had been sunk in an accident, but the first on which there was no loss of life. The impact point on the submarine's hull can clearly be seen just aft of the conning tower.

C.34 showing modifications incorporated in later boats of the class: the casing runs the full length of the hull forward of the conning tower, and it has a permanent bridge structure and a single periscope. *C.34* was lost on 17 July 1917 when she was torpedoed by *U52*, east of Fair Isle.

C.17 under way at Spithead shortly after completion. *C.17* was the first submarine built for the Navy by the Royal Dockyard at Chatham, and thus the monopoly which Vickers had held over submarine construction since *Holland 1* was broken. Chatham Dockyard went on to build 55 submarines for the Royal Navy, the last being HMS *Ocelot*, launched in 1962. *C.17* also had a larger bridge structure than earlier boats in the series, although it provided little or no shelter from the elements. *C.17* conducted the first submarine beach reconnaissance at Middlekerke in Belgium. In 1917 she was ordered to measure the tidal rise and fall off the beaches in preparation for a proposed amphibious assault on the coast, to coincide with the Army's third offensive at Ypres. *C.17* set off from Dover and simply lay at the bottom while the commanding officer, Lieutenant Wardell-Yerburgh, used the submarine's depth gauge to measure the rise and fall of the tide. The submarine was dived for a total of thirty-six hours and even though she had sailed with a reduced complement, many of the crew were half dead with carbon dioxide poisoning when she eventually surfaced.

C.29 leaving Portsmouth in 1909. *C.29* was one of four 'C' class submarines involved in anti U-boat operations off the east coast of Britain in 1915. The submarine was towed and submerged by a trawler which acted as a decoy. The U-boat would surface to sink the trawler by gunfire and was then attacked and sunk by the submarine. A telephone line attached to the towing cable allowed for communication between the trawler and the submarine. The scheme actually worked: *U23* and *U40* were both sunk by this method. *C.29* was lost on 29 August 1915 when her towing trawler *Ariadne* strayed into a mined area off the Outer Dowsing Light Vessel on the Humber. Those on the *Ariadne* were horrified to see a huge explosion astern of them. The loss of *C.29* marked the end of the trawler/submarine partnership.

With the exception of the three boats at Hong Kong and the two boats sent to the Mediterranean in 1918 for anti-submarine work, the Cs were employed exclusively in home waters. However, in August 1916 *C.26*, *C.27*, *C.32* and *C.35* were sent to the Baltic to reinforce the 'E' class submarines operating there. The submarines were towed to Archangel and then made their way down the White Sea Canal on lighters to Kronstadt where they were prepared for short patrols in the Gulf of Riga. This photograph shows *C.35* on her lighter on arrival at Kronstadt. It also gives an extremely good view of the casing built on the spindle-shaped hull to give the submarine a more 'ship shape' for improved handling when on the surface.

The four Cs had very brief careers in the Baltic. *C.32* grounded in Vaist Bay in Estonia and on 22 October 1917 was blown up to avoid capture. The remaining three boats were scuttled in Helsingfors Bay, Finland, on 4 and 5 April 1918 when the decision was taken to withdraw the British from the Baltic following the Russian revolution and subsequent Bolshevik takeover. This photograph shows the three Cs at Helsingfors being prepared for scuttling.

C.3 was selected for an apocalyptic end in 1918. As part of the raid on Zeebrugge the submarine, commanded by Lieutenant Richard Sandford and packed with high explosive, was rammed under the viaduct which connected the mole with the mainland, thus preventing the arrival of German reinforcements while the main assault went ahead. Even though the viaduct was heavily guarded, Sandford succeeded in placing *C.3* in position before he and the five members of the crew made their escape in a small skiff while under fire from the German guards. From a distance they were able to witness the explosion of the 5 ton charge which blew the hole in the viaduct shown in the photograph. For this action, Sandford was awarded the Victoria Cross.

German seaplanes strafing *C.25* during her ordeal on 6 July 1918 off Harwich. The seaplanes were returning from a raid on Lowestoft and opened fire on *C.25* with machine guns, killing the commanding officer, Lieutenant David Bell RN, and fatally wounding the other three men on the bridge. One of the three survivors, Leading Seaman William Barge, shouted to the first lieutenant, 'Dive Sir! Don't worry about me – I'm done for, anyway.' But the first lieutenant, Sub Lieutenant Roland Cobb RN, struggled onto the bridge and dragged Barge down the hatch to the control room where he died as he was laid on the deck.

C.25 on the surface and unable to dive, surrounded by shell splashes. Inside the submarine the crew were frantically trying to plug the many holes in the hull. However, when Cobb gave the order to dive, he found that the lower conning tower hatch would not shut because the leg of one of the bodies on the bridge was jamming it. Two men were killed trying to free the hatch before Cobb sawed the limb off. Help arrived in the shape of the submarine *E.51* but she was forced to dive when another five German aircraft appeared. Eventually the destroyer HMS *Lurcher* arrived and drove the aircraft off. Leaking like a sieve and with her control resembling an abattoir, *C.25* was towed back to Harwich.

D.1 goes down the ways at Barrow on 16 May 1908. Her launch was conducted with little of the ceremony which usually attends such occasions. The Admiralty's caution was justified as *D.1* represented a considerable advance on previous classes of submarine. The Ds were the first British submarines to have external ballast tanks (which gave far greater space inside the hull), twin screws (which gave greater manoeuvrability), and diesel engines which were more reliable and meant an end to the foul petrol fumes that had made life so unpleasant in the previous classes. The Ds were the first submarines to be fitted with WCs or 'heads', as they were more popularly known.

A view of a 'D' class submarine in dry dock. The external ballast tanks on the side of the hull are clearly visible. In the Ds the forward two torpedo tubes were mounted one above the other. This arrangement gave improved seakeeping qualities as the bow had a finer shape, but it made the task of loading the upper tube inside the cramped interior extremely difficult. The manhole-like fitting under the hydroplanes housed the 'drop weight' anchor, which could be operated while the boat was dived.

D.1 under way in the Solent shortly after completion. The Ds were the first submarines to be fitted with wireless telegraphy (W/T): the aerial can be seen strung from the mast on the bridge to the stump mast at the bow. The capabilities of this new submarine were quickly shown by her young CO, Lieutenant Noel Lawrence, in the 1910 Manouevres when he 'torpedoed' two of the opposing fleet's cruisers. Another young submarine CO, Lieutenant Max Horton, penetrated the defences of the Firth of Forth in D.2 and 'torpedoed' his own depot ship. Both these officers were to make names for themselves in the First World War, in which three of the eight Ds were sunk.

D.5, seen here leaving Portsmouth, was the first of the class to be lost when she was mined off Yarmouth on 3 November 1914. Along with *D.3* and *E.10*, *D.5* had been ordered to sea to intercept units of the German High Seas Fleet returning from a bombardment of Yarmouth. Shortly after getting under way, *D.5* was mined aft and sunk quickly, leaving her commanding officer, Lieutenant Godfrey Herbert, and four others to be picked up by the trawler *Faithfull*. The sinking of *D.5* was the fourth of five submarine accidents in which Herbert was involved.

'Just back from the Heligoland Bight.' A filthy but cheerful member of *D.2*'s crew on return from patrol in the autumn of 1914. In November 1914 *D.2* became the fourth British submarine to be lost when she failed to return from a patrol of Borkum. There were no survivors.

All the Ds served in Home Waters during the First World War and to a certain extent their operations have been overshadowed by the following 'E' class. Nevertheless, they had their moments: *D.4*, seen here before the war, had a narrow escape on 22 June 1915 when she attacked the German minelayer *Bielefeld* which had gone aground in the Heligoland Bight. Her CO, Lieutenant Moncreiffe, decided to sink the destroyer that was standing by the grounded minelayer before sinking *Bielefeld*. However, the torpedo missed and *D.4* found herself being hunted in very shallow water – the depth showing on the depth gauge was 30 ft. The destroyer made repeated runs over the submarine, evidently trying to ram the conning tower, and Moncreiffe and his crew could do nothing but hope for the best. Eventually the destroyer made off and Moncreiffe was able to surface and sink the *Bielefeld*.

E.1 leaving Portsmouth. This submarine was the first of a class of fifty-seven submarines which formed the backbone of the British submarine fleet throughout the First World War and of which twenty-nine were lost. *E.1* was one of the first group of the class (*E.1* to *E.9*) which were basically enlarged 'D' class submarines in which the armament was rearranged to give single bow and stern tubes and two beam tubes firing port and starboard. *E.1* was one of five boats to penetrate the Baltic where she damaged the German battlecruiser *Moltke* on 19 August 1915. *E.1* was eventually scuttled on 3 April 1918 at Helsingfors to prevent her falling into the hands of the Bolsheviks.

AE.2, one of two Es built for the Australian government, was despatched to the Dardanelles as part of the Imperial contribution to the war effort. There she became the first submarine to pass through the nets and minefields of the Dardanelles and enter the Sea of Marmara on 25 April 1915. However, five days later she was sunk by the Turkish destroyer *Sultanhissar*.

E.4 at Harwich in the early days of the war with an unusual armament of four 6 pounders on high angle mountings, a sure sign that German Zeppelins were making their presence felt. The gun was to play an important role in submarine operations, both as a means of self-defence and as a weapon used to sink small targets not worth a torpedo. *E.4* was commanded by one of the great characters of the early Submarine Service, Lieutenant E.W. Leir, known as the 'Arch Thief' who plundered His Majesty's Navy of anything portable and of whom it was said that only his DSC was earned honestly! *E.4* was subsequently lost with all hands in a collision with *E.41* on 15 August 1916.

E.22 with two Sopwith Schneider seaplanes on her after casing. The seaplanes were intended for use in operations against German Zeppelins which were making a nuisance of themselves off the east coast of Britain, and for bombing Zeppelin bases. To launch the seaplanes the submarine trimmed down and the aircraft floated away to take off under their own power. Recovery was equally simple: the seaplane landed alongside the submarine and was assisted back onto the casing while the boat lay trimmed down. It was an ingenious scheme but impractical. The seaplanes could only be launched in very calm weather and the submarine could not dive without jettisoning the aircraft. *E.22* never used her Sopwiths operationally and she herself was torpedoed in the North Sea by *UB18* on 25 April 1916. The remains of her 'flight deck' were used by the survivors to keep themselves afloat until they were rescued.

E.9 in wintry conditions at Reval in the Baltic, February 1915. Five Es (*E.1, E.8, E.9, E.18* and *E.19*) entered the Baltic to support the Russians although the latter had not been consulted about the deployment and thus expressed some surprise when the first British boats arrived at Reval.

E.13 interned in Copenhagen by the Danes and showing the effects of German shellfire. The boat was en route for the Baltic but had run aground near the Danish island of Saltholm on 18 August 1915 due to a faulty gyrocompass. Her CO, Lieutenant G. Layton, was warned by the Danes that he had twenty-four hours to refloat the submarine or be interned. A German torpedo boat *G132* was also observing proceedings but did not interfere. However, two more German torpedo boats appeared and began to shell the helpless submarine. Fourteen members of her crew were killed or subsequently died of their wounds and the casualty list would have been bigger were it not for the Danish torpedo boat *Soulven* who placed herself between the submarine and her assailants.

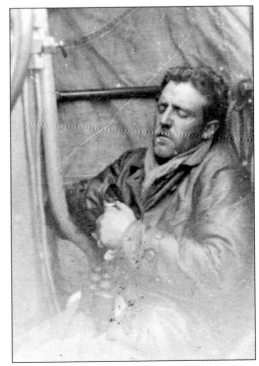

Lieutenant Alexander Greig, first lieutenant of *E.8*, asleep on the bridge in 1916. Sleep was a precious commodity and an opportunity to snatch a quick nap was not wasted even in the most uncomfortable surroundings.

A more formal photograph of Greig with his CO, Commander Francis Goodhart, after the latter had been invested with the St George's Cross by Tsar Nicholas II on 10 November 1915 for sinking the German cruiser *Prinz Adalbert*. The Tsar subsequently inspected *E.8* which had been cleaned up for the visit, although the occasion was marred by one of the imperial suite managing to fall down the periscope well in the boat's control room.

Revolution. The Russian imperial ensign is hauled down on the depot ship *Pamiat Azova* at Reval in October 1917 to be replaced a short time later by the Red Flag. Note the Es lying alongside the depot ship's starboard side. While Russia remained in the war, the British submariners continued in their operations against the Germans though hampered by the weather and the growing political instability throughout the country. It was only after the Bolshevik seizure of power that the submariners scuttled their boats and returned to the UK. Commander F.N.A. Cromie, the senior submarine officer, remained in the USSR attached to the British embassy in Moscow. He was murdered by a Bolshevik mob on 31 August 1918.

E.15 aground in the Dardanelles after trying to enter the Sea of Marmara on 17 April 1915. She had grounded in full view of Turkish shore defences and was subsequently disabled by gunfire. Her CO, Lieutenant C.G. Brodie RN, was killed while leaving the conning tower. The Turks attempted to salvage the submarine but her hull was subsequently destroyed by torpedoes fired by British picket boats.

Author's Collection

E.14 (Lieutenant Commander E.C. Boyle) at Mudros, about to sail for the Sea of Marmara. *E.14* was the third British submarine to attempt the voyage but was the first to return. *E.15* was sunk on her inward journey, while the Australian *AE.2* was sunk in the Marmara before she could return. Boyle spent twenty-two days in the Marmara and on his return was immediaely awarded the Victoria Cross. *E.14* had two commanding officers in her brief life and both were awarded the VC. After Boyle left the submarine, she was commanded by Lieutenant Commander G.S. White who was posthumously awarded the VC for an attempt to sink the German battlecruiser *Goeben* in the Dardanelles in January 1918.

E.11's crew pose for the photographer on the casing after their return to Mudros on 7 June 1915 following the completion of the second. Damage to one of the periscopes can be seen. This was sustained on 23 May 1915 in an engagement with the Turkish gunboat *Peleng I Derya*. Nasmith despatched the gunboat with a torpedo but the crew continued to fire at *E.11's* periscope as their ship sank beneath them. One shell took a neat piece out of the periscope and for the rest of the patrol Nasmith had to operate with only one periscope. *E.11's* second patrol lasted from 5 August to 2 September and was crowned by the sinking of the Turkish battleship *Heireddin Barbarossa* on 8 August.

Lieutenant Commander E. de B. Stocks standing by *E.2*'s collapsed 12 pounder mounting after her return to Mudros on 14 September 1915 following a patrol in the Marmara. The mounting became caught in nets during the passage up the Dardanelles and was badly strained as a result. Two days' hard work were required before the gun was serviceable. Then in an action against a Turkish Q ship with *E.11*, the mounting collapsed, but *E.2*'s engine room department was able to make such repairs that enabled the submarine to bombard the port at Mudania in another joint operation with *E.11*.

E.7 (Lieutenant Commander A.D. Cochrane) sails from Mudros on her second and last patrol in the Marmara. While proceeding up the Narrows by Nagara Point, the submarine became entangled in a net and could not break free. The commotion on the surface caused by Cochrane's manoeuvring of his submarine did not go unnoticed. A spectator of events was *Oberleutnant zur See* Heino von Heimburg, commanding officer of a German U-boat under repair at Chanak. Heimburg himself visited the spot in a small skiff (rowed by his cook) and lowered a small explosive charge over the side. When he made contact with what he hoped was a submarine, he fired the charge and was rewarded with the sight of *E.7* coming to the surface. Cochrane and his crew became prisoners of war (although Cochrane escaped in 1918) and Heimburg dined out on the story for the rest of his life!

The crew of *E.20* pose proudly with their new submarine at Barrow in 1915. *E.20* went out to the Dardanelles armed with a 6 inch howitzer (just visible on the casing) which was for use in shore bombardments. She successfully negotiated the Narrows, but her rendezvous with the French submarine *Turquoise* inside the Marmara was compromised. The latter boat had been abandoned and no effort had been made to destroy confidential books and papers. As a result when *E.20* reached the rendezvous, she met the German *UB14* which despatched her with a single torpedo on 6 November 1916.

E.31 under construction at Scotts yard in 1915. *E.31* was a member of the much larger second group in which the armament was increased by the addition of a second bow tube. Provision was also made for carrying one 12 pounder gun on the casing. Other improvements included a larger conning tower, a third watertight bulkhead and a 'plough' type bow to improve seakeeping. In this photograph the submarine is partially completed with some frames on the pressure hull and saddle tanks still exposed. The framework for the casing on top of the pressure hull is also visible.

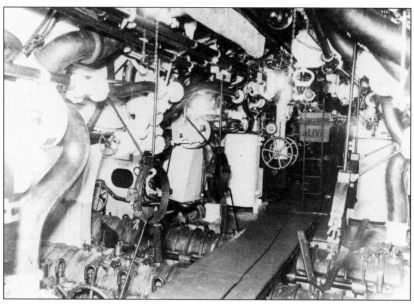

The two midships beam torpedo tubes in *E.31* seen looking forward into the control room. The tubes themselves are covered by planking and above the tubes are the collars for holding the re-load torpedoes. The ladder in the background leads up to the lower conning tower hatch and then to the bridge. The submarine's wheel is to the left of the ladder.

The crew of *E.34* on the casing and conning tower at Harwich shortly before the submarine was lost, probably mined, on or around 20 July 1918. Her CO, Lieutenant R.I. Pulleyne, seen on the conning tower, was the only survivor from *B.2*'s collision with the *Amerika* in 1912. *E.24*, *E.34*, *E.41*, *E.45*, *E.46* and *E.51* were configured as minelayers, carrying twenty mines in ten vertical chutes (two per chute) in the saddle tanks, five on each side. Considerable structural modifications were required to fit the mine wells and the beam torpedo tubes were omitted in these submarines.

A mine of the type used by the 'E' class minelayers (and the late 'L' class minelayers) about to be lowered down into the chute. With the exception of *E.46*, the minelayers operated in home waters where they were used to harass U-boats using supposedly safe routes to and from patrol. *E.46* went to the Adriatic to do the same sort of work against German and Austrian U-boats operating from Cattaro. However, the depth of water in that area was too great for her mines to be effective.

Definitely the most hazardous job in a minelaying submarine! The coxswain in an 'E' class minelayer uses a long pole to check that the mines have released after an operation and that none are 'hung up' in the chutes. Given that the mines were loaded with their contact horns upwards, this was a task which required some delicacy and not a little nerve!

E.55 on completion. She represents the final stage in the development of the Es. Improvements to the basic design included a screen around the conning tower, folding W/T masts (which can be seen in the 'down' position on the side of the casing), sky searchers fitted to the periscopes so that a check could be made for hostile aircraft before surfacing, sounding machines, Fessenden and water jet signalling equipment and last, but by no means least, WCs that could be blown at depth. Built by Denny in 1916, *E.55* was sold for breaking up in September 1922.

The 1912 Submarine Development Committee

In October 1910 Captain Roger Keyes was appointed as Inspecting Captain of Submarines. Keyes had never been one of the Navy's intellectuals or 'technocrats' but he was an officer with imagination, flair and a drive for getting things done. His previous appointment had been as naval attaché in Rome and thus he was acutely aware of the progress made in submarine design and construction in Europe. Keyes felt that Vickers had the monopoly in the development of British submarine design and that important developments overseas, particularly in the field of double-hull submarines where the ballast tanks were contained between an inner and outer hull, should be noted. Accordingly, Keyes sponsored a committee which examined foreign designs, made recommendations for the design of 'coastal' and 'overseas' submarines and invited companies other than Vickers to submit their own designs. The membership of this committee consisted of six officers:

Commander P. Addison, Commander C. Little, Lieutenant Commander N.F. Laurence, Lieutenant Commander M. Dunbar-Nasmith, Lieutenant Commander C. Craven and Engineer Commander L.W.R. Skelton. In time, the first four names reached flag rank and headed the Submarine Service. Lieutenant Comm-ander Craven became Managing Director of Vickers Armstrongs and Engineer Commander Skelton became Engineer in Chief of the Navy. Whatever Keyes' shortcomings, there was no shortage of skill or expertise among his advisers. The committee, known as the Submarine Development Committee, reported in 1912 and recommended that the Navy pursue the development of two distinct types of submarine: a small type for operations in coastal waters and a larger overseas type. The committee also recommended studying foreign designs to see what could be learned and incorporated into British practice.

The result was a proliferation of different designs being built. Four types of coastal submarine entered service: the Ss, built by Scotts to an Italian design, the Ws, built by Armstrongs to a French design, the Vs, which were an in-house Vickers' design and the Fs, which were an Admiralty design. Without exception these submarines proved unsuitable for British service. The Ss and the Ws lacked the seakeeping qualities required for operations in the North Sea and were eventually transferred to Italy. The Fs and the Vs were regulated to training duties.

As regards the overseas type of submarine, the Navy ran up against the fact that diesel development was still in its infancy. The first large submarine, *Nautilus* or *N.1*, built by Vickers, was twice the size of any other submarine in British service, yet her diesel engines gave but a small increase in speed only: three knots over an 'E' class submarine. The Glasgow firm of Scotts, which had built the 'S' class under licence from Laurenti, suggested that the solution lay in the introduction of steam propulsion which would generate the extra speed required. The result was *Swordfish*, the first steam-powered submarine in British service. At the same time as Keyes was investigating building bigger and faster submarines, intelligence reached Britain of German submarines which were capable of extremely high speeds on the surface. Although these rumours were false, they set a British programme in motion to build submarines of a similar performance. These were the boats of the 'G' and 'J' classes, which incorporated many of the

features advocated by the 1912 Submarine Development Committee but used existing machinery for their propulsion. Both were useful types and rendered valuable war service.

The search for a submarine with a high surface speed was given further stimulus in 1915 with a requirement from the Grand Fleet for a submarine which could run ahead of the battle fleet, carry out reconnaissance, launch attacks on the enemy battle fleet and be around to finish off any cripples afterwards. Thus was born the 'fleet submarine': a submarine capable of operating as an integral part of the fleet. This doctrine flew in the face of all the experience gained in pre-war exercises, when it proved extremely difficult to coordinate the movements of ships and submarines, and early war experience. In the early days of the war there had been a number of 'near misses' between British ships and submarines working in the same area.

The Gs and Js were never fast enough to be really effective in the scouting role; the top speed of a J was supposed to be 21 knots but in practice they never exceeded 19 knots. The result of this continuing requirement was the 'K' class steam-driven submarine. Described by one observer as the 'result of an unholy union between a destroyer and a submarine', the Ks acquired an unenviable reputation for accidents. Eight suffered disasters, and there were sixteen major accidents together with an untold number of mishaps. Yet the construction and introduction of the Ks represented an enormous technological achievement and the submarines matched the speeds demanded of them. It was not this concept that was flawed, rather the ships and submarines of the day lacked the effective communications to make it work successfully. Tragic proof of these inadequacies came in the so-called Battle of May Island on 31 January 1918 when two Ks were sunk and three others badly damaged in a series of collisions.

Three other classes of submarine made their appearance during the First World War: the 'H', 'R' and 'L'. The Hs were an American design bought 'off the shelf' as a means of increasing the number of submarines in commission. Although intended as a short-term measure, some Hs were in service thirty years later in the Second World War. The Rs were specialist anti-submarine boats, the first submarines to be purpose-built for these operations. Lastly, the Ls were a good basic design and are the true successors to the 'E' class and thus represent a return to a line of development which had begun with *Holland 1*.

The boats and designs resulting from the 1912 Submarine Development Committee occupy an important place in the history of the Submarine Service. The lessons learned from the opening up of the design and construction process were of immense value. The boats themselves were less useful. For all Keyes' efforts in 1914, the bulk of the British submarine fleet was made up of the As, Bs and Cs; only eighteen boats of the 'D' and 'E' classes were in commission. On the other hand, the Germans had twenty-eight boats, comparable to the Ds and Es in commission and another twenty-eight under construction. Keyes' efforts merely dissipated submarine strength on a motley collection of foreign designs which were no better than anything produced by Vickers. The construction of the large steam-driven 'K' class was a superlative technological achievement, but it is hard to justify the resources poured into their development when the country was engaged in total war with Germany. It is important to remember that while Keyes was experimenting with new and exciting designs the 'E' class construction programme – which provided the Navy with a good workmanlike submarine which bore the brunt of wartime operations – virtually ground to a halt. In later life Keyes recalled that, 'I do not think that material is my strong point,' although a more appropriate verdict might be the one given by Admiral Sir Geoffrey Layton, who commanded *K.6*, that, 'Keyes made a b**** of the submarine programme.'

Scotts was first off the mark with the four boats of the 'S' class built to an Italian Fiat San Giorgio design; this photograph shows *S.1* on trials off Gourock. This was a coastal submarine with a double hull of 265/324 tons with an armament of two 18 inch torpedoes. An interesting feature of the design was that the 'S' class had no fewer than ten internal bulkheads; a Group One E boat only had two.

S.1 had one adventure before her transfer to Italy. On 21 June 1915, while on patrol north of Heligoland under the command of Lieutenant Commander Gilbert Kellett, the submarine's port engine broke down. This was soon followed by the failure of the starboard engine. The boat was unable to charge the battery and her prospects looked grim. Three days later Kellett sighted the German trawler *Ost* and sent over a boarding party. The *Ost* then took the submarine in tow and eventually returned to Yarmouth, though not before *S.1*'s engineers had to turn their attentions to the *Ost*'s overworked engine!

V.1 was one of a class of four submarines designed and built by Vickers as a rival to the Scotts design. The Vs were a useful design although their underwater endurance was very low.

W.2 goes past the battleship HMS *Canada* on the Tyne after completion in 1914. The four Ws were built by Armstrongs to a French Schneider Laubeuf design: her French ancestry is very evident in the shape of the hull. After a visit to Toulon, the British decided against the French design but four such boats were ordered as a result of a promise to Armstrongs to order two boats (any boats) a year from the company. The Ws suffered the same fate as the Ss and were transferred to Italy in 1916.

F.2 on trials in the Solent in 1917. The three Fs were an Admiralty design and very similar to the Vs. However, they carried an additional stern tube. The Fs were perhaps the least successful of the four designs of coastal submarine and were largely relegated to training duties.

As well as the requirement for small coastal submarines, the 1912 Submarine Development Committee also laid down a requirement for a large ocean-going submarine capable of high surface speeds. This boat, *Nautilus* (the first British submarine to be named), seen here at Barrow on completion, was the first manifestation of that requirement. She was supposed to be capable of a surface speed of 20 knots but her diesels never developed sufficient power. As a result she was neglected and relegated to training duties having abandoned her name in favour of the more prosaic *N.1*. *Nautilus* has generally received a bad press from historians who have ignored the fact that her construction was a considerable achievement. With a displacement of 1,441 tons, she was more than double the size of an 'E' class, the largest British boat built to date and she provided much useful data for future construction.

Swordfish's oil-fired Yarrow boiler lowered into position while the boat was under construction. *Swordfish*'s designers, acting on advice from their Italian co-designers, opted for steam propulsion. *Swordfish* had twin screws driven by one set of geared Parsons impulse reaction turbines. Boiler exhaust was vented through a hydraulically operated funnel located just aft of the bridge. Naturally, the steam plant could not be used while the boat was dived and the funnel was yet another opening in the pressure hull which had to be checked before diving. Though *Swordfish* was not a success operationally, she provided much useful experience for the next class of steam-driven submarines, the Ks.

A 'G' class boat, sadly unidentified, in rough weather on patrol in the North Sea. The fourteen Gs spent the war in home waters serving with the 11th Submarine Flotilla at Blyth and the 10th at South Bank on the Tees. Some of the class also spent time operating from the Kola Inlet in north Russia with the light cruiser *Fearless* as their depot ship. Three were lost on patrol: G.7, which disappeared on or around 1 November 1918, was the last British submarine to be lost in the First World War. The rough weather shown in the photograph is typical of conditions in the North Sea and which prompted the comment of one submarine CO, on being asked what he had seen while on patrol, 'Nothing but water and a damn sight too much of that.'

A rare view of *G.2* in dry dock. The open aperture for the port side beam tube can be seen in the bulge on the submarine's side. The camouflage pattern was intended to make the submarine less visible from the air as well as to break up the boat's silhouette when on the surface. A number of famous artists, including Norman Wilkinson, were involved in the design of such schemes.

The control room of *G.5*. The hydroplane wheels and depth gauges are in the centre of the photograph. The commanding officer's bunk is behind the curtains in the background while the first lieutenant slept behind the depth gauges and hydroplane wheels; the end of his bunk can just be seen at the right-hand side. The equipment enclosed within the wire cage is the Fessenden underwater signalling apparatus which could be used to communicate with other ships or submarines using sound: a precursor of the modern SST.

G.10 alongside the depot ship *Titania* at Blyth in April 1916. While engaged in exercises the submarine paid the price for failing to keep a good all-round lookout. A merchant ship passing through the exercise area rammed the submarine's bridge. The bridge was reduced to a shambles and both periscopes were wrecked: minor damage when considering what might have been the result of such an encounter. One of the merchant ship's propellers was later found embedded in the wreckage and, after removal, was mounted above the dockyard gates as a warning to the unwary!

J.1 in the basin at Portsmouth on completion. The 'J' class were larger than the 'G' class and were built to answer a requirement from the Grand Fleet for a submarine with a high surface speed capable of operating with the fleet in a scouting role. Since two shafts could not develop sufficient power, the Js became the Royal Navy's only submarines to be fitted with three shafts. They had two engine rooms and machinery occupied 36 per cent of the hull length. The Js were also armed with a bow salvo of four 18 inch tubes, the first submarines to be thus fitted. The very fine shape of the bow (a requirement for the high surface speed) meant that there was insufficient space in the bow for each tube to have individually operated bow caps and shutters. A mechanism was therefore developed (which proved very successful) for the bow cap and shutter to be operated as one. The Js were regarded as the *ne plus ultra* of the submarine service at the time and the commanding officers appointed to the first boats, Laurence, Horton and Nasmith among others, were the élite of the Submarine Service.

Author's Collection

A splendid view of *J.5* on completion. Although the Js never achieved the speeds required of them by the Grand Fleet, they could make 19.5 knots in the heaviest seas. *J.5* is shown here with a raised bow, a design modification to improve seakeeping.

The Js were fitted with a 4 inch gun mounted on a 'disappearing' mounting which recessed into the casing. Here, Commander Max Horton, *J.6*'s commanding officer, watches the gun being raised into the operating position. Having the gun in a recessed mounting was intended to reduce underwater resistance, but it increased the time taken to bring the gun to action and secure it afterwards. Nevertheless, 'disappearing' guns were to remain a feature of British submarine design until the early S boat designs of the 1930s.

Commander Noel Laurence, the first commanding officer of *J.1*. In early November 1916, units of the High Seas Fleet sortied to give cover to salvage vessels attempting to salve the wreck of *U20* which had gone aground. The British learned of what was afoot through intercepted wireless transmissions and *J.1* was diverted from patrol and ordered to intercept the Germans. Laurence sighted the German force on 5 November and, in a determined attack carried out in heavy swell which made depth-keeping extremely difficult, hit and damaged the battleships *Kronprinz* and *Grosser Kurfurst* with one salvo. Though both ships were badly damaged they managed to return to harbour. Nevertheless, the attack is unique in submarine history: no other commander before or since has hit two capital ships in a single salvo.

J.1 in modified form with the 4 inch gun in a fixed mounting ahead of the bridge. After her service in the North Sea the Submarine was transferred to Gibraltar where she was employed in anti-submarine patrols in the Eastern Atlantic and Western Mediterranean. *J.1* was unique in that she was fitted with depth charges which 'launched' through vertical tubes (operated by a volunteer crew under the direction of the chief stoker) which had inner and outer watertight doors. Once loaded, the inner door was shut and the outer door opened, the depth charge literally dropped and the submarine went to full speed to escape the worst effects of the explosion. On 9 November 1918 *J.1* (Lieutenant Commander Frederick Kennedy RN) sighted the German *UB57* passing westward through the straits. Kennedy opened fire with the gun and then, ordering the chief stoker to stand by, ran over the spot where the U-boat had dived and dropped one depth charge. *UB57* escaped but, nevertheless, the attack is another unique occasion in submarine history.

Author's Collection

J.4 passing through the Suez Canal in 1919. Australian troops are lining the canal banks to give the boat a tumultuous passage. Note the awnings spread along the full length of the casing against the heat. The Js were offered to Australia after the First World War as part of Britain's contribution to increased imperial defence in the Far East. The boats served throughout the 1920s, but all had been broken up by 1930.

J.7 in Plymouth Sound on completion. *J.7* had a different layout to the others in the class in that the control room was placed aft of the machinery spaces. This arrangement, with the bridge and conning tower 60 ft further aft than usual, gave the boat a curiously elongated appearance.

K.6 on builder's trials in Plymouth Sound. This submarine demonstrated the accident-prone nature of the class by obstinately refusing to surface for hours during a dive in a non-tidal basin in Devonport Dockyard. A subsequent enquiry could find no reason why the submarine failed to surface. Dockyard workers then refused to board the submarine for further trials.

The same submarine in 1918 after a refit in which the bow was raised to improve seakeeping qualities. Behind the submarine are battleships of the 5th Battle Squadron, ships which the Ks were designed to support through reconnaissance. Interestingly, at the left-hand side of the photograph is the aircraft carrier HMS *Argus*, another new addition to the fleet.

A view of the four 18 inch bow tubes of *K.8* showing the lower two torpedoes partly withdrawn for the daily maintenance routine. Spare torpedoes can be seen in the loading racks on either side. In addition to these bow tubes, the Ks carried four beam tubes and a twin revolving mounting in the casing.

K.22 preparing to dive, showing the funnels partly retracted into their housing in the casing. This boat once attempted to dive with her funnels raised and with potentially disastrous consequences. With over forty vent valves involved, diving took a long time (3 minutes 25 seconds was the fastest time recorded, although 5 minutes was nearer the norm, compared with an H-boat's 30 seconds) and had to be done carefully so that the tanks were flooded evenly. With a length to beam ratio of 12.8:1 the Ks were very difficult to control when dived and if a bow-up or bow-down angle developed it was very difficult to rectify since the broad casing acted as a huge hydroplane, causing the boat to see-saw. In deep water their unhandiness could prove fatal: a diving depth of 61 m and a length of 100.6 m meant that the bow could be at the crush depth in seconds if the dive was a steep one. Such was probably the fate of *K.5*, lost on 20 January 1921.

The bows of the cruiser HMS *Fearless* photographed at Rosyth in February 1918. On the night of 31 January 1918 nine Ks put to sea with units of the Grand Fleet for an exercise. *K.22* collided with *K.14* whose helm had jammed while avoiding some minesweepers which had not been warned of the fleet's approach. Minutes later, *K.22* was rammed by the battlecruiser HMS *Inflexible*. In the resulting confusion *K.17* was rammed by *Fearless* and *K.4* was rammed by *K.6* and *K.7*. *K.17* and *K.4* were sunk with the loss of over one hundred lives and the others were damaged to various degrees. The incident was known as the Battle of May Island and led to some criticism of the K boat's officers by the Admiralty. However, the correct view, quoted by one of the participants, was that the Ks came to grief because they had, 'the speed of a destroyer, the turning circle of a battleship and the bridge control facilities of a picket boat'.

K.26 under way in the Mediterranean in 1928 with her crew cheering Admiral Sir Roger Keyes on the occasion of his relinquishing command of the Mediterranean Fleet. It was an appropriate farewell for an officer who had done much to bring the 'K' class into service. *K.26* was built to a modified design which included an enhanced gun armament of three 4 inch guns and the fitting of 21 inch torpedoes. Even so, she was not immune from the bad luck which dogged her sisters: on one occasion two stokers were killed when relief valves in the boiler room failed when she was raising steam. *K.26* was the only one of a class of six to be built and she was eventually broken up in 1931.

The remarkable *M.1* under way in the Firth of Forth on completion. The four 'M' class boats were built on the hulls of *K.19–K.21*. Their construction was cloaked in secrecy and at one time work was suspended for fear that the Germans would learn of their design and build an equivalent boat. The 'M' class was unique in that they were armed with a 12 inch gun taken from a redundant 'King Edward VII' class battleship. The theory was that the boat would surface and loose off one or two rounds at the enemy before diving. However, the submarines lacked the fire control equipment to operate the gun at maximum range, so the idea was flawed. *M.1* was despatched to the Mediterranean where plans existed for either a bombardment of the Austrian base at Cattaro or a forced passage to the Dardanelles to bombard Constantinople. This latter plan must have been regarded very dimly by her ship's company and fortunately the war ended before it could be put into action.

M.1's wardroom with a genial Commander Max Horton sitting at the table. The size of the Ms meant that the officers' accommodation was comparatively spacious. The Ms betrayed none of their 'K' boat ancestry: they were easy to handle, both dived and on the surface. The bulk of the 12 inch gun helped the submarine in diving yet the volume of the mounting helped to stabilize the boat at periscope depth.

M.1 firing her 12 inch gun off Gibraltar in 1923. On this occasion, water had leaked into the barrel while the boat was dived. When the gun was fired the shell took most of the muzzle with it, still secured to the wire winding between the inner and outer jacket.

M.2 in her revised configuration as an aircraft-carrying submarine and with the Parnall Peto airborne after leaving the catapult. The aircraft was used for reconnaissance purposes but the tactical disadvantages of such a system are obvious. The submarine had to remain on the surface during the launch and recovery period and thus was extremely vulnerable to detection and counter-attack.

M.2 was lost with all hands on 26 January 1932 during exercises off Weymouth. It is believed that seawater flooded into the hangar after the door had been prematurely opened while the submarine was surfacing but had not attained full buoyancy. This photograph shows how easily such an incident could happen. The boat has just surfaced and the 'flight deck' party (some of whom would have been RAF personnel) are checking the catapult. The submarine is not at full buoyancy and the sea is creeping perilously around the hangar entrance. Inside the hangar a 16 inch coaming was supposed to prevent water flooding down into the control room, but on the occasion of the submarine's loss, the flood of water into the hangar must have been too great. Subsequent examination of the wreck showed that both the hangar door and the hatch leading from the hangar to the control room were open.

M.3, last of the trio, was converted to a minelayer and carried eighty Type B mines on a track laid inside her large casing. *M.3*'s conversion was perhaps the most successful of the three and she provided much useful experience which was later used in the 'Porpoise' class minelayers. Ironically, as soon as the submarine demonstrated the validity of the concept, she was placed for disposal and sold for breaking up in 1932.

The first four submarines of the 'H' class at St John's, Newfoundland, in 1915. As part of the massive wartime expansion of the submarine fleet, the Admiralty ordered ten submarines from the Bethlem Steel Company as part of a large arms contract worth $15 million. The boats were assembled by Canadian Vickers in Montreal from parts made by Bethlem in the US; this arrangement neatly side-stepped American neutrality laws.

H.1 under way during her Atlantic crossing to the UK. The H-boats were a single-hull design and suffered from a very low reserve of buoyancy. Note the guard rails fitted, the raised W/T mast and the canvas dodger fitted to the bridge. The figure seated forward of the conning tower is the submarine's CO, Lieutenant Wilfrid Pirie. *H.1* made patrols in the sea of Marmara, but spent the rest of the war in the Adriatic on anti-U-boat patrols off the port of Cattaro. On 16 April 1918 she sank a 'sister' submarine, the Italian *H.5*, also built by Canadian Vickers. The Italian boat had strayed out of position and into *H.1*'s area with the inevitable and tragic consequences.

Six 'H' class submarines (*H.5* to *H.10*) preparing for their Atlantic crossing. Laid down in January 1915 these boats were completed in six months. As with *H.1* to *H.4*, the boats were assembled in Montreal by Canadian Vickers from parts prefabricated in the United States. However, a second batch of ten boats that were ordered direct from Fore River were impounded by the US government, which warned that the boats would not be delivered until the war was over. In the event, the boats were delivered in 1917 when America entered the war. But by then the British 'H' class programme was under way, so six of the boats were given to Chile as compensation for Chilean warships seized in British yards in 1914 on the outbreak of war.

H.8 coming alongside the depot ship HMS *Maidstone* showing damage to her casing caused when she struck a mine while dived on 22 March 1916. Fortunately, the pressure hull was not damaged and her CO, Lieutenant B.L. Johnson RNR was able to bring the boat back safely.

Lieutenant Cromwell H. Varley in seagoing rig. Varley commanded *H.5* and brought her across the Atlantic from Montreal in 1915. On 14 July 1916 he sank *U51* in a well-executed attack off the Jade River and survived the inevitable counter-attack. However, his achievement did not receive the usual recognition accorded such incidents. Varley had incurred their Lordship's displeasure when he left his assigned patrol area because he was 'bored and wished to sink a submarine'. Varley was a skilled engineer and during the Second World War was closely involved with the development of the X-Craft midget submarine.

H.49 under way on completion. Twenty-two 'H' class submarines were built in British yards following the American embargo. The original order was for thirty-four boats but this was reduced after the Armistice. They were slightly longer than the US-built boats and armed with the bigger 21 inch torpedo tube. Despite the problems inherent in a single-hull design, the 'H' class were very successful and some survived to make operational patrols in the Second World War.

A truly rural scene. *H.33* observed by a cyclist and a couple out with their dog, passes along the Sharpness–Gloucester Ship Canal through the West Country scenery. *H.33* was accompanied by *H.49* whose CO, Lieutenant J. Collett, had arranged the visit to his home county.

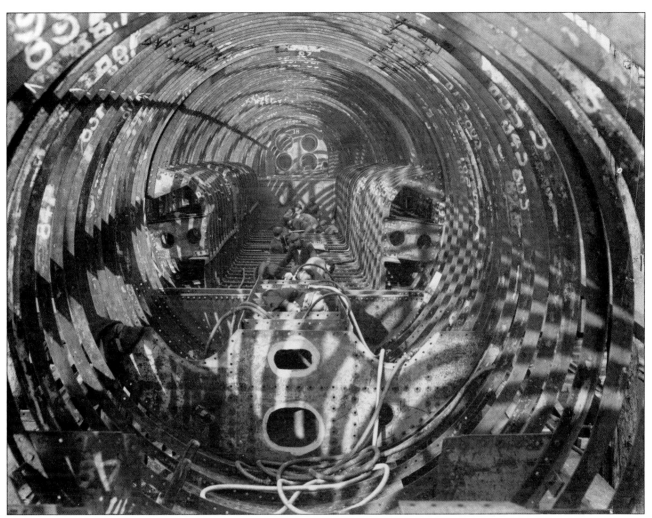

Inside an 'H' class submarine under construction and looking forward along the boat from aft. The apertures for the 21 inch torpedo tubes can be seen at the far end of the boat. The workmen in the midships portion are working on the battery section. Because of the single-hull design, the main and auxiliary ballast tanks were placed under the battery; the tops of the tanks extended up and beside the battery section, as can be seen in the photograph.

Toilet facilities in early submarines were very primitive and did not improve much thereafter. The sole 'throne' for ratings in *H.43* was located at the after end of the engine room between the thrust blocks. Anyone using it had to do so in full view of the engine room watchkeepers. This particular photograph shows the officers' heads in *H.43* which were located in the control room. Space being at a premium, the seat was also used by the signalman who was responsible for keeping a log of events during an attack.

Loading 21 inch torpedoes into *H.43* at Portland. Every 'H' boat carried a small crane for this evolution which could be stowed in the casing when not required. Embarking torpedoes was a task which called for a considerable amount of hard work and brute strength from the crew, but also required a degree of delicate manouevring. It was not easy guiding the torpedo down the fore hatch and onto its cradle in the fore ends.

H.42 on the surface and being taken into tow by the cruiser HMS *Curacao* following her collision with the destroyer *Vancouver* on 9 February 1922 during the combined Home and Mediterranean Fleets' manoeuvres. Damage to the submarine's conning tower is clearly visible. One month later *H.42* was not so lucky. On 23 March 1922 she was rammed and sunk with all hands by the destroyer HMS *Versatile*.

L.8 on completion. The 'L' class were the true successors to the 'E' class after all the diversification and distractions resulting from the 1912 Submarine Development Committee. The Ls were larger and faster than the Es but retained the same armament. All the boats carried a gun on the forward casing; the 4 inch was eventually fitted as a standard weapon but before that a variety of weapons were carried. *L.1*, for example, carried a 3 inch HA gun on a 'disappearing' mounting. *L.8* is shown unarmed in this photograph but the sponson for the gun on the casing is visible.

L.18, one of the second group of 'L' class submarines (*L.9* to *L.49*, although only eighteen were completed) on which the 4 inch gun was mounted at bridge level. This arrangement meant that the gun could be brought into action without waiting for the submarine to gain full buoyancy and that the gun could be worked in rough weather without the danger of the crew being washed over the side. This arrangement was retrospectively fitted to the earlier submarines of the class. Another alteration in the design was that the 21 inch torpedo tube replaced the 18 inch form on the bow tubes, although the latter was retained for the beam tubes. Unusually, the Ls were fitted with three periscopes: the third, fitted in between the search and attack periscope, was for night work.

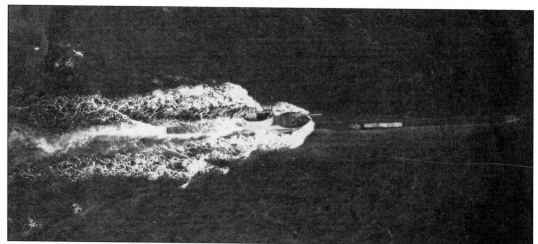

L.10 diving during trials to determine how visible a submarine was underwater, taking into account various conditions of light and depth. Even though only the submarine's gun platform is awash, the forward casing is visible underwater. *L.10* was the only one of the class to be lost during the First World War. On 30 October 1918 she attacked a force of four German destroyers and torpedoed the German destroyer *S33* which had stopped to rescue survivors from her sister ship *S34*, which had struck a mine. The Germans thought that *S33* had been mined as well but these thoughts were dispelled when *L.10* broached, doubtless having lost trim on firing. The German ships lost no time in opening fire and *L.10* was hit several times, sinking with no survivors.

L.5, showing the gun sited on the bridge, trimmed down by the bow alongside the depot ship *Ambrose* at Wei-hei-wei in China. The absence of any docking facilities meant that simple repairs to the propellers, rudder or after hydroplanes were often carried out by the simple means of flooding the boat's forward ballast tanks, thus raising the stern.

Chief Petty Officer E.F. Buck, coxswain of *L.3*, photographed on the China Station, 1919–21. Buck later joined *L.24* and was lost with her when she was rammed and sunk by the battleship *Resolution* on 10 February 1924. Buck's son was not deterred by his father's death for he too served in submarines throughout the Second World War.

A fine view of *L.56* at Malta, 1925–6. *L.54*, *L.56*, *L.69* and *L.71* had their after 4 inch gun replaced with a dome to house the oscillator for a 113C ASDIC set. It was strongly felt by some submariners in the inter-war period that the growing efficiency of escorts in anti-submarine work meant that it would not be possible in a future war to get close enough to a target to aim the torpedoes entirely by eye. Instead, a submarine would fire from long range using ASDIC information to supplement visual observation and fire a large salvo of torpedoes. This argument eventually matured with the 'T' class with their massive bow salvo of ten 21 inch torpedo tubes. However, when the set was used in the active mode its transmissions were of more use to the 'opposition' in locating the submarine than vice versa. Nevertheless, the Type 113C proved very efficient in the passive listening role.

R.4 under way just after the First World War. *R.4* was one of a class of eight submarines specially designed for anti-submarine operations. The design was unique and years ahead of its time in that their underwater top speed of 15 knots was greater than their surface speed. *R.4* served in a training role at Portland until 1934. Her nickname of 'The Slug' testifies to her streamlined form, although the single screw made manouevring on the surface difficult.

The business end of *R.8* showing her six 18 inch torpedo tubes. Apart from *K.26*, the 'R' class carried the heaviest armament of any British submarine in the First World War. The wooden cabinet on the port side aft of the tube space contained the hydrophone equipment: an unusually comprehensive array of five hydrophones which, it was claimed, could be used to track a target without use of the periscope.

Three submarines alongside at Fort Blockhouse illustrate the state of British submarine development at the end of the First World War. Inboard is *L.12*, an overseas saddle-tank type submarine. In the middle is *H.28*, a single-hull coastal submarine, while outboard is *R.7*, designed exclusively for anti-submarine operations. The 'R' class was soon discarded, a victim of the economies demanded of the Navy in the inter-war period, but the 'H' and 'L' classes went on to form the backbone of the inter-war submarine fleet.

THE INTER-WAR
YEARS

The first task confronting the Submarine Service in the period immediately following the First World War was the drastic reduction in boats and manpower as a result of cuts demanded by the government. In practice this meant that all surviving boats of the 'A', 'B', 'C', 'D', 'E', 'F', 'G' and 'V' classes would be paid off while the 'J' class were sent to Australia.

The first submarine to be built to a new design in the inter-war period reflected new priorities and a new task for the Submarine Service. *Oberon*, launched in 1924 and commissioned in 1926, was the first of nineteen broadly similar submarines built in four classes, designed for long-range operations in the Far East. Before and during the First World War Japan had acted as Britain's policeman in the Far East, leaving Britain free to concentrate resources against Germany. After the First World War Britain, anxious to avoid another lethally expensive naval race and under pressure from the United States, cancelled this agreement and thus became solely responsible for the security of her possessions in the Far East.

There was no way that Britain could afford to maintain a battle fleet in home waters and a separate one in the Far East. Instead, the bases at Singapore and Hong Kong were developed while the planners at home devised ways and means (most either impractical or unaffordable) as to how the forces in the Far East could be reinforced should the political situation there deteriorate. In the meantime Britain's naval interests in the Far East were represented by a cruiser squadron, a destroyer flotilla, a submarine flotilla and numerous smaller vessels. Only the submarines were capable of inflicting serious damage on the Japanese fleet and thus the submarines of the 4th Flotilla became Britain's main line of defence in the Far East.

When war broke out in September 1939, the 'O', 'P' and 'R' classes were stationed in China. There they remained to protect British possessions (although their operations included intelligence gathering in Japanese and Soviet waters) until the summer of 1940. Then, on Italy's declaration of war, they were transferred to the Mediterranean. It was not a theatre to which their large size was suited. Of the nineteen boats in the group, one (*Poseidon*) was sunk in a peacetime accident, another (*Oxley*) was torpedoed in error off Norway, twelve were sunk in the Mediterranean and only five survived the war.

HMS *Oberon*, launched in 1926 and the first post-war submarine design which was based on the successful *L.9* group. With a displacement of 1598/1831 she represented a considerable increase in size on previous boats. She was armed with eight 21 inch torpedo tubes (six bow, two stern) and a 4 inch gun. Extra fuel, essential for the long passages on the Far Eastern station, was carried in external riveted fuel tanks which leaked atrociously when the hull started working. *Oberon* soon acquired a reputation for mechanical unreliability and the nickname HMS '*Oh be Joyful*' due to the amount of time she spent in dockyard hands with her crew being given leave far more often than usual.

Two modified Oberons, *Oxley* and *Otway* were built for the Royal Australian Navy but were handed back to Britain in 1931; this photograph shows *Oxley*. A distinguishing feature of these two boats is the ram bow and that they carried their hydroplanes beneath the waterline. *Oxley* was the first British submarine to be sunk during the Second World War when she was torpedoed in error by HMS *Triton* off the Norwegian coast on 10 September 1939. *Oxley* had inadvertently gone out of her patrol area and into *Triton*'s. When challenged by the latter, one mistake in a chapter of accidents meant that she did not reply to *Triton*'s challenge and was thus taken for a U-boat and sunk. Only one rating and her commanding officer survived.

Otus photographed in Plymouth Sound in 1930. Note the very tall W/T mast, essential for communications in the Far East. *Otus* was one of six boats similar to *Oberon*, but they had the advantage of more powerful engines and were fitted with above-water hydroplanes. The six boats spent virtually their entire lives on the China Station but were transferred to the Mediterranean in 1940, a theatre for which they were not particularly suited. *Otus* and *Osiris* were the only ones to survive the war.

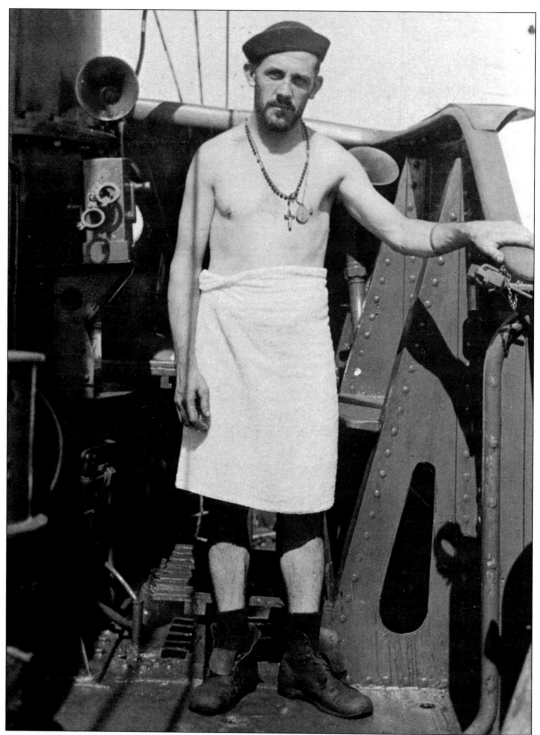

Able Seaman 'Daisy' Adams in informal rig on *Orpheus*'s bridge in the Far East in the 1930s. The rig of towel and boots was not unknown when off duty in the tropics.

Osiris's crew at Beirut in April 1943 on their return from patrol. On 22 September 1940, *Osiris* sank the Italian destroyer *Palestro* off Brindisi. On hearing the torpedo strike, *Osiris*'s commanding officer, Lt. Cdr. J. R. 'Ginger' Harvey, is alleged to have said, 'F**k me, I've hit it!'

The 'O' class were followed by six units of the 'P' class which were broadly similar in design. This is *Perseus* shown during her work-up before proceeding to China. The torpedo-loading derrick is rigged indicating that the submarine may be about to recover torpedoes fired on exercises. *Perseus* was one of three submarines initially armed with the 4.7 inch gun for trial purposes which was eventually replaced by the standard 4 inch weapon. *Perseus* was mined off Zante on 6 December 1941: there was one survivor, Leading Stoker Capes, who escaped from the sunken submarine

HMS *Pandora*'s water-polo team, 1936. The pre-war submarine service was a small tightly-knit community and the casualties suffered in the Second World War were deeply felt. Of the nine men in this photograph, only three survived the war. Back row, left to right: Petty Officer (LTO) C.G.H. Duffay (killed in *Triumph* in December 1941), Leading Stoker J.A. Abraham (invalided from the Service in January 1939), Stoker J.I. King (killed in *Triton* in December 1940), Able Seaman D. Allen (also killed in *Triton*), Leading Seaman C.J. Thomas (survived after completing patrols in *Rorqual*, *Parthian* and *Sealion*). Front row: Stoker Petty Officer F. Lowe (killed in *Thunderbolt* in March 1943), Lieutenant R.D. Cayley RN (commanded *Utmost* with distinction and was killed in command of *P.311*), Warrant Engineer A. Giordan (survived), Able Seaman G.H. Mellows (lost in *Snapper* in February 1941).

Phoenix's gun crew photographed in 1934 with the trophy for the annual Captain (S) Firing Competition. This was a timed gunnery exercise in which the submarine surfaced from periscope depth, fired ten rounds at a target and submerged again. The submarine was timed on the time taken from the signal being given to surface and the first round being fired and then all ten rounds. The number of hits was also counted. In this case, the first round was away 25 seconds after the order to surface was given and the whole exercise only took 1 minute and 5 seconds, with seven hits scored out of ten. No wonder Lieutenant Commander L.L.B. Myers, *Phoenix*'s commanding officer (seated left) looks pleased. Success in such exercises were important steps on an officer's path to promotion.

Proteus was the most successful of the 'P' class in war as is shown by the Jolly Roger displayed on the submarine's return to England in October 1943. The 'tin opener' featured in the bottom left corner was the result of an encounter with the Italian torpedo boat *Sagittario* on 8 February 1942. *Proteus*'s captain thought the *Sagittario* was a submarine and, after he failed to hit her with a torpedo, surfaced and tried to ram her. When he realized that the target was a warship he turned away, but in doing so *Proteus*'s hydroplanes tore a gash in the *Sagittario*'s side. Ironically, many of the ship's company were later drafted to HMS *Tally Ho!* and were to endure a similar experience in the Far East.

Rainbow on the China Station in the 1930s. To prevent 'misunderstandings' with the Japanese Navy, which was active in Chinese waters supporting Army operations ashore, British submarines had identification letters painted prominently on the conning tower. The principle difference between the 'R' class and their predecessors was that their conning tower and gun position were slightly lower. All four Rs were lost during the Second World War. *Rainbow* was sunk in collision with an Italian merchant ship, *Regent* and *Regulus* were mined and *Rover* was damaged in an air attack on Crete in 1941; she spent the rest of the war staggering from port to port in search of a refit.

The bridge, gun and forecastle of HMS *Rainbow* during operations in the North Pacific in January 1940 where she operated as far north as Vladivostok. Thick ice formed on the periscope standards and the W/T aerial was carried away under the strain of bearing too much ice. The greatest concern was that the boat would be prevented from diving owing to partial freezing of the telemotor system. Although there was 'peace' in the Far East for nearly two years after the declaration of the war in Europe, the Japanese attitude was openly hostile and Soviet Russia's was ambivalent. Thus, submarines of the 4th Flotilla conducted aggressive intelligence-gathering patrols in Japanese and Soviet waters.

The sixteen submarines of the 'O', 'P' and 'R' classes represented a steady if unspectacular stream of development to which the submarine *X.1* was an exception. This vast 2,780/3,600 ton submarine was armed with four 5.2 inch guns designed for long-range surface operations and carried a gun armament sufficient for her to take on a destroyer. Though she was undoubtedly well armed, as well as the guns she carried six 21 inch torpedo tubes, her designers seem to have forgotten that one hit on her pressure hull would have been fatal. Submarines are not designed to slug it out with surface ships.

Disaster struck on 26 June 1931 when *X.1* was under refit in No. 15 dock at Portsmouth. The wooden shoring on the port side collapsed and the submarine slipped over onto her port side. After a career bedevilled by mechanical unreliability, *X.1* was broken up in 1936. Although her machinery gave endless problems there is evidence, suppressed at the time, that she would have been successful in the commerce-raiding role. Britain, with the largest merchant fleet in the world, had nothing to gain if this knowledge were made public so *X.1* was consigned to scrap.

TOWARDS ANOTHER WORLD WAR

During the second decade of the inter-war period, submarine construction was dominated by two considerations: the limits placed on submarine construction by the 1930 and 1935 London Naval Treaties and the British government's plan to secure the total abolition of the submarine by treaty.

The naval disarmament treaties placed individual and total tonnage limits on submarine construction. Under the terms of the 1930 London Naval Treaty, Britain was restricted to a total tonnage of 52,700 tons and individual boats were restricted to a maximum of 2,000 tons and to carry a gun no greater than 5.1 inch size. The Admiralty believed that the next disarmament conference, to be held in 1935, would place further limits on submarine construction. The Americans were demanding an individual limit of 1,200 tons while the British government was proposing that the submarine be abolished altogether. The Admiralty was fairly certain that this proposal would not

be accepted and so was able to be fairly confident regarding future construction.

These restrictions were of considerable importance when designing the submarine to replace the 'O', 'P' and 'R' classes. The new submarine, known as the 'Replace P', would have to be capable of the same endurance but be markedly smaller in view of forthcoming treaty restrictions. In the event, the second London Naval Treaty left individual tonnage and armament figures for submarines unaltered but, in the absence of Japan (which had withdrawn from the international system of arms limitation), it proved impossible to agree on quantative limits. To all intents and purposes international regulation by naval armaments by treaty was over.

Nevertheless, the design work on the 'Replace P' had been done with such limits in mind and what emerged was the 'T' class submarine. These boats, of which fifty-three were eventually built, were undoubtedly the finest submarines ever constructed for the Royal Navy. Their main role against surface units of the

Japanese fleet was emphasized in their armament: ten, formidable, forward-facing 21 inch torpedo tubes. For their time they had a very high standard of accommodation and every man onboard had his own bunk. The 'T' class were to serve the Navy well for over thirty years and proved themselves capable of absorbing a large number of modifications made as a result of war experience.

Four other classes of submarine also entered service during this period. The 'S' class were small coastal submarines intended for operations in the coastal waters around the UK and in the Mediterranean. The 'U' class were intended as unarmed training submarines to replace the 'H' class. As Britain re-armed in the late 1930s six, then four, torpedo tubes were worked into the design. The 'U' class did sterling work in the Mediterranean, working from Malta, in sinking supply ships taking supplies to the Axis armies in North Africa.

Britain also continued to show an interest in the fleet submarine. Three boats of the 'River' class were built (out of a projected twenty) which carried the same armament as an *Oberon*. Even though the experience of the First World War had shown that the concept of the fleet submarine was fallacious, not to mention downright dangerous, the concept was revived in the inter-war period. Eventually it was the restrictions placed on submarine construction by international disarmament treaties and financial economies imposed by the government which sounded the death knell for this type of submarine.

The six minelayers of the 'Porpoise' class adopted the minelaying system first tested in the short-lived *M.3*. They were designed for offensive minelaying operations in the Far East. They proved exceptionally successful in service and operated as conventional patrol submarines as well as in the minelaying role, but also made a sterling contribution to the relief of Malta by carrying stores to the island at the height of the siege. Only *Rorqual* survived the war.

The boats of the 'S', 'T' and 'U' classes bore the brunt of submarine operations during the Second World War and their war was unlike that fought by submariners of any other nation. On the whole, British submarines worked in shallow coastal waters strewn with minefields (the extent of Axis minelaying was only really appreciated after the war) and close to enemy bases with their concentrations of ASW forces. Targets were few and invariably heavily escorted. Given these circumstances, the successes achieved by British submarines were remarkable. In home waters, their activities were the only redeeming feature of the Norwegian campaign and, for the rest of the war, German capital ships in Norwegian waters could only move under heavy escort. The Mediterranean, with its clear and shallow water, was not the ideal environment for underwater operations but it was here that British submarines made their most important contribution to the war effort. Operating from Malta, despite the intensity of the Axis air offensive, as well as from Gibraltar and Alexandria, they savaged Rommel's supply routes and prevented the adequate reinforcement of the Axis armies in North Africa at the time of the Battle of El Alamein. Submarine operations in the Far East had to take a back seat until sufficient boats could be released from commitments in home waters and the Mediterranean. British pre-war plans for this theatre had not envisaged the speedy fall of the bases at Singapore and Hong Kong. Consequently, British submarines were committed to long passages from their new bases in Ceylon and Australia to their patrol areas.

From 1939 to 1945 British submarines sank 493 enemy merchant ships totalling 1,524,000 g.r.t. and damaged another 109 ships (518,000 g.r.t.); to these figures must be added the 35 enemy ships destroyed by submarine-laid mines. Results against enemy warships were equally satisfying:

6 cruisers, 16 destroyers, 34 submarines and 112 other warships were sunk, while 2 battleships, 10 cruisers, 2 destroyers, 6 submarines and 35 other warships were damaged. Another 6 enemy warships fell victim to submarine-laid mines.

The price of these successes was high: 75 of the 215 submarines that served in the Royal Navy did not return from patrol (35%) while 3,142 submariners were killed and another 360 were made prisoner of war (out of approximately 25,000 men in the Submarine Service). Winston Churchill paid eloquent tribute to the Submariners when he said, 'Of all branches of men in the forces, there is none which shows more devotion and faces grimmer perils than the submariner . . . Great deeds are done in the air and on land, nevertheless nothing surpasses your exploits.'

HMS *Thames*, one of three 'River' class submarines designed with a high surface speed, 22 knots, to enable them to operate with a surface squadron. This high speed was obtained by fitting the diesels with mechanical superchargers which developed a total of 10,000 b.h.p. It was planned that twenty of this class would be built, but the plans were shelved. These were large submarines with a displacement of 2,206/2,723 tons, but their armament of only six 21 inch torpedo tubes gave them a very poor armament to weight ratio. *Thames* was mined off Norway in July 1940. *Severn* and *Clyde* survived the war. Although they never participated in the fleet operations for which they were designed, they proved particularly useful when engaged in store-carrying operations to Malta and in special operations, landing special forces and their supplies, in the Far East.

Vice Admiral Sir Cecil Talbot with his two sons. Talbot had been the first submariner to win the DSO while in command of *E.6* in the First World War. Both his sons followed him into the Submarine Service and both lost their lives in the Second World War: Lieutenant F.R.C. Talbot (left, shown when a Sub Lieutenant) was killed in *Thames* in July 1940; Lieutenant E.B. Talbot was killed in *Snapper* in February 1941.

HMS *Porpoise* in the Devonshire Dock at Barrow on completion in 1933. *Porpoise* was a submarine minelayer and carried fifty Mk XIV mines inside the casing on top of the pressure hull. The mines were loaded onto an 'endless chain' and laid via doors in the stern. *Porpoise* was a single-hull saddle-tank design with most of her fuel carried in external welded tanks. The step in the forward casing is a feature unique to *Porpoise*.

A view of *Narwhal*'s stern taken at Immingham in 1940 showing one Mk XVI mine on the casing and another framed in the mine hatch at the stern. Minelaying was a task which called for skilful manipulation of the submarine's internal ballasting arrangement. As each mine was laid, an equivalent amount of water had to be taken on board in order to compensate for the loss of weight. Failure to do this correctly would mean the submarine losing trim and possibly breaking surface in full view of the opposition.

Porpoise approaches the quayside at Manoel Island, Malta in 1942. The minelayers proved extremely useful when employed in store-carrying operations to Malta since a considerable quantity of stores could be carried in the mine casing. Such stores included spare torpedoes, ammunition, cased petrol (on one occasion in *Rorqual* the fumes from cased petrol were so strong that the use of pyrotechnic recognition signals was forbidden), food, essential stores and dried baby milk. On arrival at Malta the stores would be disembarked extremely quickly so that the submarine spent the minimum amount of time alongside.

Porpoise's crew display two Jolly Rogers on their return to the UK from the Mediterranean in December 1942. The flag on the right shows six ships sunk by torpedo and one successful gun action. The mine symbol represents the number of minelays carried out by the submarine. The flag on the left with the initials PCS (Porpoise Carrier Service) refers to her store-carrying operations: nine successful return trips.

A cheerful group of ratings onboard HMS *Seal* in 1940. *Seal* struck a mine while on a minelaying operation in the Kattegat on 4 May 1940. Although she was badly damaged, her crew succeeded in bringing her back to the surface. Her CO, Lieutenant Commander Rupert Lonsdale, decided to head for Sweden and internment, but they were attacked en route by German aircraft. The submarine could not dive and was barely manoeuvrable on the surface and, moreover, Lonsdale and his crew were suffering the effects of carbon dioxide poisoning due to their long dive. Lonsdale took the difficult but correct decision to surrender: a decision that was subsequently upheld by the Admiralty.

Author's Collection

Seal was commissioned into the *Kriegsmarine* as *UB*; this photograph shows her commissioning ceremony at Kiel. Although *Seal*'s crew had done their best to wreck the submarine before going into captivity, the Germans succeeded in bringing her into harbour. They made much of their new prize for propaganda purposes but she was never put into service. Her eventual fate is unclear: she was abandoned by the Germans when they had no further use for her and her hull was later damaged in an RAF raid on Kiel, where her rusting remains were found when the town was captured in May 1945.

HMS *Rorqual* at Malta in 1943. *Rorqual* was the most successful of the minelayers, laying a total of 1,284 mines, and the only one to survive the war.

Inside *Rorqual*'s control room in 1941. The commanding officer, Lieutenant Commander L.W. Napier, is using the periscope. The photograph shows how the CO is crammed in against the hull of the submarine because the periscopes are offset to starboard. The periscopes, normally situated on the centre line of the submarine, were offset to allow the minetrack to run the full length of the hull.

Rorqual's fore ends showing the rear doors of two of the six 21 inch torpedo tubes. *Rorqual* was extremely successful when acting as a conventional submarine in operations in the Adriatic, despite her large size. Note the safety forks from torpedoes which struck a target, hanging on the bulkhead, one of them commemorates the sinking of the Italian submarine *Pier Capponi*, south of Stromboli on 31 March 1941.

HMS *Sturgeon* photographed just after completion in 1933. *Sturgeon* was one of sixty 'S' class submarines built between 1931 and 1945. They were designed for short-range operations in coastal waters to replace the 'H' class submarines which were nearing the end of their service lives. Great importance was attached to a quick diving time (20 to 30 seconds), mechanical reliability, and manoeuvrability both on the surface and submerged. They carried an armament of six 21 inch torpedo tubes (the same armament as *Thames* but on a hull of only 640/927 tons) and a 3 inch gun.

Swordfish and *Starfish* moored in St Katherine's Dock for the 1937 coronation celebrations. The 'S' class were single-hull saddle-tank submarines in which all fuel was carried in internal tanks.

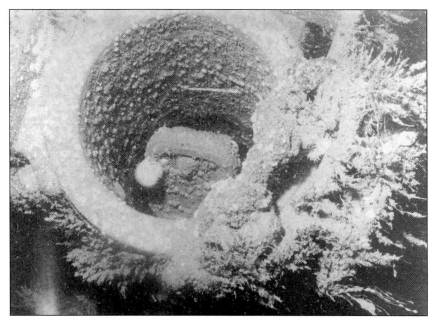

Swordfish disappeared in November 1940 after sailing from Portsmouth for a patrol off Ushant. It was presumed that she had been lost in her patrol area until July 1983 when her wreck was found off the Isle of Wight. Examination of the wreck showed that she had been mined. This photograph shows the top of the periscope standards. The rectangular upper lens of the search periscope can be seen in its housing.

Salmon was lost off Norway – probably mined – in July 1940 but in less than a year she had run up an impressive tally of victims. On 4 December 1939 she torpedoed *U36* and on 13 December 1939 she hit and damaged the cruisers *Leipzig* and *Nurnberg*. There were no survivors when *Salmon* was mined and thus the Navy lost one of its most promising commanding officers, Commander E.O. Bickford, DSO.

On 5 July 1940 HMS *Shark* was attacked in the Skaggerak by an aircraft with depth charges. The submarine was damaged and unable to dive and was then subjected to repeated air attacks for over eighteen hours during which three of her crew were killed and eighteen wounded. Eventually *Shark*'s CO, Lieutenant Peter Buckley, realized that there was no hope and surrendered. This photograph shows *Shark*'s crew mustered on the casing while a German A/S trawler prepares to take the submarine in tow. However, *Shark*'s crew had made a thorough job of wrecking the boat and she sank before the Germans could save her.

Sunfish was transferred to the USSR in 1944 and renamed *V.1*. Here her old British and new Soviet crews pose for the photographer after the handover at Rosyth. Less than a month after this photograph was taken *V.1* was sunk in error by an RAF Liberator; a subsequent enquiry revealed that the submarine had strayed from the safe route allocated to her. War losses among the first twelve 'S' class were high: only *Sturgeon* and *Seawolf* survived the war.

HMS *Saracen*, seen here in Algiers in February 1943, was one of a group of thirty-three improved 'S' class submarines ordered under the 1941 War Emergency Programme. Apart from being slightly larger, the main difference was that the *Saracen* and her sisters were fitted with an external torpedo tube (one that could not be reloaded from inside the submarine) facing aft to give a much-needed stern salvo. On her working-up patrol *Saracen* sank *U335* and then went on to sink the Italian submarine *Granito* in the Mediterranean. Her war came to an end on 14 August 1943 when she was depth-charged by the Italian corvettes *Minerva* and *Euterpe*.

HMS *Satyr*, another Group 2 'S' class submarine, showing the other principle wartime modification, the addition of a 20 mm Oerlikon gun in a bandstand mounting at the after end of the conning tower. From 1943 onwards all new-construction submarines were destined for the Far East. To give the submarines the extra endurance required for the long voyages between their bases and their patrol areas, two of the main ballast tanks were converted to carry oil fuel, thus increasing the fuel carried from 45 to 67 tons. Further modifications meant that another 25 tons could be accommodated.

HMS *Safari*'s ship's company show off their Jolly Roger on their return to Portsmouth from the Mediterranean on 8 September 1943. Under the command of Commander 'Ben' Bryant and Lieutenant R.B. Lakin, *Safari* (perhaps the best known of the 'S' class) sank a considerable amount of Axis shipping.

One of *Safari*'s victims burns after being shelled in the Gulf of Policastro on the Italian coast in January 1943. Note how close to the shore the action is taking place. Bryant was a keen exponent of using the 3 inch gun to sink targets which were not worthy of torpedoes. Although an unrepentant advocate of the gun, Bryant was bitterly critical of the shortcomings of the 3 inch compared with the more powerful 4 inch.

Stubborn returns to Greenock on 25 February 1944 after an epic ordeal off Norway. On 13 February she had attacked a convoy and was then severely depth-charged by the escorts. Over seventy depth-charges were dropped and she was forced down to a depth of 540 ft; her test depth was 300 ft. The submarine was eventually able to surface but was damaged and perilously exposed off an enemy coast. Virtually the whole Home Fleet was mobilized to bring her home. She then proceeded to Scapa Flow and secured alongside the battleship HMS *Duke of York*, flagship of the Commander in Chief Home Fleet, Admiral Sir Bruce Fraser. When she cast off the next day Fraser signalled, 'I was proud to have laid alongside you in my flagship.'

Another highly decorated Jolly Roger, this one belonged to HMS *Seraph*. *Seraph* participated in a number of special operations including, briefly, assuming the identity of an American submarine (a disguise which fooled nobody) when she took General Mark Clark of the US Army to a covert meeting with French generals in North Africa before operation *Torch*. *Seraph* was later involved in an operation to deceive the Germans about Allied strategy in the Mediterranean in which a body, dressed as a major in the Royal Marines and carrying a briefcase packed with carefully forged documents, was put into the sea off the Spanish port of Huelva, safe in the knowledge that the tides would wash the body ashore. Once ashore the Spanish authorities granted the *abwehr* a sight of the papers before returning them to the British. The operation was later featured in the book and film, *The Man Who Never Was*.

HMS *Stratagem* on completion. *Stratagem* was one of only three British submarines to be lost in the Far East. After sinking an escorted merchant ship on 22 November 1944 in the Malacca Strait, she was counter-attacked and suffered severe damage. Only ten men were able to escape from the submarine and of these only three survived Japanese captivity, the others being executed or dying as a result of the appalling conditions.

HMS *Shakespeare*, seen here in Algiers in 1943, had one of the most harrowing experiences of any British submarine during the Second World War. On 3 January 1945 she was badly damaged off Port Blair at the northern end of the Malacca Strait after an engagement with a Japanese escort. Her pressure hull was holed and she was unable to dive. The submarine began the long voyage back to Trincomalee on the surface.

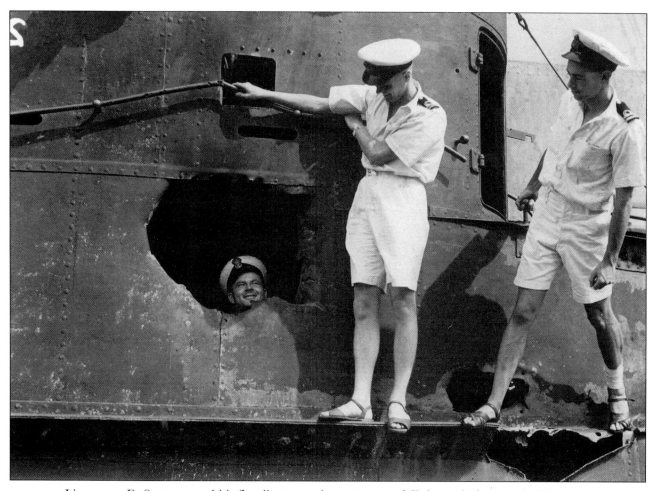

Lieutenant D. Swanton and his first lieutenant inspect some of *Shakespeare*'s damage; in this case a hole in the starboard side of the conning tower. The Japanese were not slow to follow up the engagement and *Shakespeare* was soon the victim of repeated air attacks which went on for some considerable time. Over twenty-five individual attacks on the submarine were recorded and fifteen of *Shakespeare*'s crew were wounded. *Shakespeare*'s wireless was destroyed, so her CO, Lieutenant D. Swanton, had to seek help and headed for the patrol area of her sister submarine, HMS *Stygian*, with the expectation that the latter could radio for assistance. *Stygian* was duly sighted on 6 January and after a cautious exchange of signals designed to confirm that *Shakespeare* had not fallen into Japanese hands, *Stygian* was able to radio for help and send over her own engineers to assist in repair work. Two days later *Shakespeare* returned to Trincomalee.

Lieutenant J.A. Troup (left) and the officers of HMS *Strongbow* at Trincomalee after their escape from a Japanese attack off Port Swettenham on 13 January 1945. *Strongbow* had been detected on the surface, possibly by a shore-based DF station homing in on transmissions from her Type 291 radar set, and escorts had been sent out to find her. *Strongbow* endured a series of damaging depth-charge attacks throughout the day, sustaining such damage that she had to come off patrol, thus rendering her unfit for further service.

HMS *Statesman*'s gun crew with the results of their handiwork burning behind them. *Statesman* sank forty-nine enemy vessels with her gun and expended over 1,200 rounds of ammunition. These operations were typical of those in the Far East.

HMS *Storm* returns to Portsmouth on 8 April 1945 after her deployment to the Far East. *Storm* was commanded by Lieutenant Commander Edward Young DSO DSC RNVR, the first officer of the Volunteer Reserve to command a submarine. His experiences have been brilliantly retold in his book *One of our Submarines*. *Storm* still wears the standard camouflage scheme for submarines operating in the Far East, consisting of light and dark green.

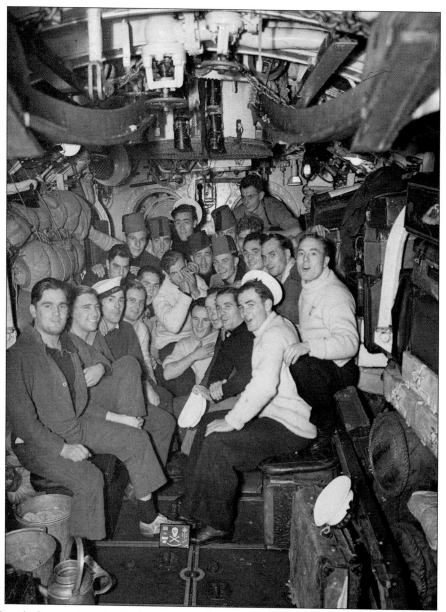

Inside *Storm*'s fore ends. The fore ends fulfilled a number of roles: workshop, torpedo stowage, accommodation and general purpose store. British submarines were not fitted with air conditioning, so conditions in the heat and humidity of the tropics were appalling. Lieutenant Commander Young admitted that, 'I felt downright ashamed of the conditions in which some of my seamen and stokers had to live.' The medical log for another submarine, HMS *Terrapin* (and there is no reason to suggest that her experiences were any different from any other submarine), shows that every man in the crew was suffering from various skin complaints: prickly heat, ulcers, not to mention cuts which turned septic and stayed septic owing to the foul conditions. There was no penicillin, only M&B antibiotic powder dispensed liberally by the coxswain together with 'Stoppage of Rum'.

On 27 February 1945 *Seadog* rescued three American airmen from a raft in the Bay of Bengal. A short while later she picked up a fourth airman who had been adrift in his Mae West for over 27 hours. The inside of the submarine was no place for airmen who had been in the sea for a considerable time, so an RAF Catalina was despatched to rendezvous with the submarine and collect the survivors. This photograph was taken from the Catalina. It shows the submarine on the surface with extra lookouts on the periscope standards and with the Oerlikon gunner closed up. The survivors are in the dinghy about to go over to the Catalina.

HMS *Sea Devil*, seen here on the Clyde in April 1945, was one of three Group 2 S boats (*Scotsman* and *Scythian* were the others) which differed from their consorts in that they were armed with a QF Mk XII 4 inch gun instead of the 3 inch. This change reflected the growing use and importance of the gun in submarine operations, particularly in the Far East where targets were few and usually not big enough to merit a torpedo. The extra weight of the 4 inch mounting was compensated for by removing the external stern tube. The dome right at the after end of *Sea Devil*'s casing is for a Type 138 ASDIC set.

A 21 inch Mk VIII** torpedo being loaded on board *Sceptre* at Holy Loch in September 1943. The torpedo weighed 3,248 lb and was 21 ft 7 in long. The warhead contained 722 lb of TNT but was later replaced by an 805 lb Torpex warhead. The weapon had a range of 5,000 yd at 45.5 knots and 7,000 yd at 41 knots. In contrast to torpedoes in other navies, notably Germany and the United States, the Mk VIII** was outstandingly reliable. The Mk VIII** continued in service after the war and was still in use some fifty-six years after the appearance of the prototype.

The 'Fruit Machine', an electrically driven mechanical fire-control computer for the torpedo armament. It was traditionally worked by the 'Fourth Hand', the most junior officer onboard, and when fed with the target's range, course and speed, together with those of the attacking submarine, determined the amount of Director Angle, where the target would be by the time the torpedo reached it. This type of machine was common to all British submarines of the Second World War. Unlike similar machines in American and German service, it did not provide a continuous solution and had to be re-set at each fresh periscope observation. Therefore, in an attack, much depended on the skill of the commanding officer.

A fine view of *Selene* proceeding down the River Mersey on completion. *Selene* was one of the seventeen Group 3 S boats of the 1942/3 Programme. These boats (with the exception of *Sturdy*, *Stygian* and *Subtle*) all carried the 4 inch gun and were thus not fitted with a stern tube. More importantly they were of welded construction. This saved weight and meant that a stronger steel could be used to build the pressure hull, thus giving a diving depth of 350 ft as opposed to 300 ft.

HMS *Truant* goes down the ways at Vickers' Barrow yard on 5 May 1939. *Truant* was one of fifty-three 'T' class which were to serve in the Royal Navy for a period of thirty-one years and which were undoubtedly the finest British submarines ever built. The 'T' class were designed against a background of treaty limitations on submarine construction and government efforts to abolish the submarine. Both the 1930 and 1936 London Naval Treaties placed limits on total and individual submarine tonnage. The designers had the difficult task of building the maximum number of seaworthy boats but staying within a total tonnage limit. It is a testament to the skill of the designers that these submarines proved so successful in service.

HMS *Tribune* goes slowly astern away from an 'S' class submarine moored alongside the depot ship *Maidstone* as she leaves Algiers for patrol in February 1943. Note the very bluff shape of the bows which was common to *Thetis, Triton, Triumph* and *Trident*. This was caused by having the hinge for the bow cap of the two bow external tubes fitted horizontally. After complaints from COs that the bluff bow caused a reduction in speed and increased diving time, the bow caps were hinged vertically, thus giving a finer shape to the bow.

HMS *Tribune* coming alongside the depot ship HMS *Forth* in Holy Loch in 1940. The submarine is flying two white ensigns, one from the top of the raised W/T mast and the other from the halyard at the after end of the conning tower. The purpose of the two flags was to leave no doubt as to the submarine's identity; accidental attacks on British submarines by 'friendly' aircraft were one feature of submarine operations which remained constant throughout the Second World War.

A remarkable photograph showing damage to *Triumph*'s bows after hitting a mine on 26 December 1939. The explosion blew off 18 ft of the submarine's bows. What is so remarkable is that all eight bow tubes were loaded and it says much for the design of the pistols that none of them exploded. One rating remained stubbornly asleep in his hammock throughout the entire affair!

HMS *Triad* on trials before the war. *Triad* was the first 'T' to be sunk in the Mediterranean, in a gun and torpedo action with the Italian submarine *Enrico Toti* on the night of 14/15 October 1940. *Triad* was the only British submarine sunk by the Italians and her loss is the only occasion in history when one submarine sank another in surface action.

Lieutenant Commander Bandino Bandini (second from the right, wearing binoculars), commanding officer of *Enrico Toti* with other members of his ship's company after sinking *Triad*.

Dott. Achille Rastelli

HMS *Thunderbolt* in Holy Loch in January 1941. *Thunderbolt* was the raised and recommissioned *Thetis* (see 'The Admiralty Regrets' section) and had been substantially modified. The principle modification was the removal of the bow external torpedo tubes which gave the bow a much finer shape as a result. Despite a certain reputation for having been the ill-fated *Thetis*, *Thunderbolt* was a happy and successful boat, sinking the Italian submarine *Tarantini* on 15 December 1940 and participating in Chariot operations. Her luck ran out on 14 March 1943 when she was depth-charged by the Italian Corvette *Cicogna*.

HMS *Tigris* in Plymouth Sound in July 1942 following a refit. *Tigris* shows nearly all of the modifications made to the early 'T' class submarines as a result of war experience: the addition of a 20 mm Oerlikon gun at the after end of the bridge and the fitting of an eleventh torpedo tube which was fitted facing aft into the after casing. The triangular DF aerial which was formerly sited at the rear has been moved onto the after casing. *Tigris* was depth-charged and sunk by the German *UJ2210* on 27 February 1943, off Capri.

The fore ends in *Tribune* showing the hideous confusion of hammocks, clothing, spare torpedoes, food (note the cornflakes lodged in the torpedo loading rails) and cooking utensils. The rear doors of six of the four internal bow tubes can be seen in the background.

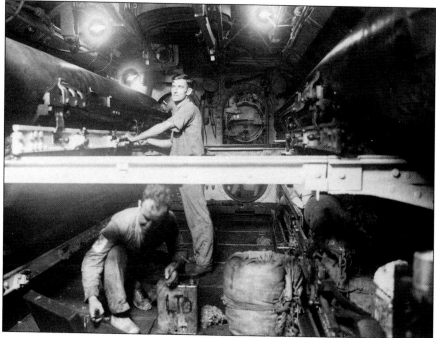

A rare photograph taken in *Traveller*'s fore ends showing the compartment rigged for loading torpedoes. The torpedoes were swung out on their trolleys on the transverse loading rails and then rammed forward into the tube. The reload torpedo for No. 2 is pulled out into the loading position.

Bunks lining the outboard side of the passageway running down *Tribune*'s starboard side. The 'T' class had been designed with the intention that every man should have his own bunk space. However, as the crew expanded from fifty-three to sixty-one to meet wartime requirements, the 'extras' either had to sling a hammock in the fore ends or 'hot bunk'.

The seamen's mess in *Tribune* with the Petty Officer supervising the hallowed daily ritual of the 'tot'. Rum was issued neat to all ratings in the Submarine Service, unlike the rest of the Navy where junior rates had theirs diluted.

The control room looking forward. The hydroplane operators' positions are on the port side and the ladder leads up to the bridge. At the forward end of the deck is the well for the binocular search periscope.

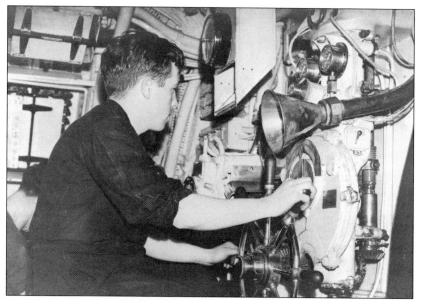

The helmsman at the lower steering position in *Tribune*. Early 'T' class submarines had one steering position on the bridge and another in the control room. The bridge position was not fitted in the boats built under wartime programmes. In front of the helmsman is the rudder indicator and the mirror shows a reflection of the magnetic compass which was mounted above the control room outside the pressure hull. The control room messenger can be seen on the left beside the boat's telephone switchboard.

Lieutenant Commander Cecil Crouch, first and only commanding officer of *Thunderbolt* at the monocular attack periscope. Behind him on his left is Lieutenant R. Bird RNVR, *Thunderbolt*'s navigator, at the chart table.

Petty Officer D.G. Waldren cleans the upper window of HMS *Taku*'s 7.5 inch attack periscope using a well-known brand of gin purloined from the wardroom. The photograph shows the very small size of the head of the periscope which was only used in the final stages of an attack.

The view looking directly up the conning tower from *Tribune*'s control room. During a quick dive by *Talisman* in April 1942, seven men and a Bren gun were crammed into this tiny space in their haste to get below. No fewer than four of the men had a part of their bodies sticking through the lower hatch.

Telegraphist Hilton sitting in *Tribune*'s wireless office which was located aft of the control room on the port side of the boat. Signals were passed to the submarine by VLF from the shore transmitter at Rugby. It was therefore mandatory for the boat to 'read' the routine transmission twice a day. The duty telegraphist would warn the CO/OOW before each transmission so that the boat would be pointed in the right direction for optimum reception; such calls could often come at very inconvenient times! The signals were received via an aerial which was strung out over the forward jumping wire and, theoretically, reception was possible while the boat was at periscope depth anywhere in the world. 'T' class were also fitted with an HF transmitting set, but this was only used with great caution for fear of enemy direction finding.

Tribune's galley with Leading Chef Beeden (left) and Telegraphist Appleton displaying their handiwork. Food was adequate but unimaginative and revolved around a few staple dishes: 'babies' heads', 'train smash', 'herrings in' and other delicacies which are now perhaps best forgotten. Even so, submariners lived like kings compared with the civilian population.

Tribune's engine room showing one of the two 6 cylinder diesels. *Tribune* was built by Scotts and thus was fitted with MAN diesels built under licence. The engines were never satisfactory and it was suggested, sarcastically, that their German designers were less forthcoming than they might have been! *Tribune* developed problems with the securing bolts for the cylinders and had to return from Canada with the cylinders held down by pit props wedged between the deckhead and the top of the cylinder. The engine room was then described as looking like 'Sherwood Forest'.

A splendid view of *Thorn* under way on the River Mersey on completion in 1941. Note the shipyard official standing rather self-consciously below the 4 inch gun. *Thorn* was one of seven Group 2 'T' class boats built to a revised design. The bows had a finer shape since the two external tubes were moved 7 ft further aft to reduce the 'hump'. *Thorn* was sunk on 7 August 1942 by the Italian destroyer escort *Pegaso*.

Traveller returning to Beirut on 1 October 1942. This photograph shows the other major modification to the Group 2 'T' class boats which was to reverse the midships external tubes so that they faced aft. With the addition of a single stern tube under casing, this gave a stern salvo of three torpedoes. *Traveller* was lost, presumed mined, in the Gulf of Taranto on or around 4 December 1942. The seven Group 2 'T' class boats all served in the Mediterranean where five of them were sunk.

Turbulent's crew with their Jolly Roger at Algiers in February 1943. Under the command of Commander J. 'Tubby' Linton, *Turbulent* was an outstandingly successful submarine as is shown by her Jolly Roger. The flag carries additional symbols for train-wrecking activities on Italy's Adriatic coast and a bombardment of a German lorry park in north Africa. Just over a month after this photograph was taken, *Turbulent* failed to return from a patrol in the Tyrrhenian Sea. Details of her fate are unclear; she may have been the victim of a depth-charge attack by the Italian destroyer *Ardito* on 6 March 1943 or she may have fallen victim to one of the many minefields around La Maddalena in Sardinia.

Commander J. 'Tubby' Linton of HMS *Turbulent* with Lieutenant Arthur Pitt, CO of HMS *Taku*. Linton was posthumously awarded the Victoria Cross for his operations in *Turbulent*, yet he remains one of the least known of the six submarine VCs of the Second World War. One of the first lieutenants said of him: 'I utterly trusted him because there was not much he didn't know about the submarine world or how to run a submarine in wartime'. Pitt said of Linton that, 'he was the most lion-hearted man I ever met'.

Commander Arthur Pitt

A view of HMS *Trooper* as modified to carry two-man human torpedoes or Chariots, two of which can be seen retracted for maintenance. *Thunderbolt* and *P.311* were similarly converted although they only carried two Chariots while *Trooper* carried three.

Thrasher in the Medway on completion of a refit. She had been fitted with radar and a 20 mm Oerlikon gun. *Thrasher* was one of eight British submarines to serve in all three theatres of war and survive. She was known to the press as the 'Double VC' boat on account of the award of two VCs to Lieutenant P. Roberts and Petty Officer N. Gould who removed two unexploded bombs from Thrasher's casing on the night of 13/14 January 1942.

HMS *P.311* on completion. *P.311* was one of the thirty Group 3 boats. Their appearance was further refined by making the casing virtually flush decked and housing the bow externals in an undignified hump on the casing. All, except for *P.311* and *Trespasser*, were built with the 20 mm Oerlikon gun. However, the greatest change in their construction was the introduction of welding, which meant that their diving depth increased from 300 to 350 ft. Fuel could also be stowed in external tanks which increased their fuel stowage from 135 to 215 tons, thus increasing their endurance to 11,000 miles – essential for operations in the Far East where most of them would be employed. *P.311* was the only T boat not to receive a name.

Commander R.D. 'Harmonica Dick' Cayley relaxing at Malta. Cayley was the first and only commanding officer of *P.311* having already commanded *Utmost* with distinction. Cayley and *P.311* were lost in January 1943 while engaged in Operation Principle, a Chariot attack on Italian cruisers at La Maddalena.

HMS *Tally-Ho!* on her way out to the Far East and passing through the Great Bitter Lakes. Under the command of Lieutenant Commander L.W.A. Bennington (one of the few wartime submarine commanders to have been promoted from the lower deck) *Tally-Ho!* sank the Japanese light cruiser *Kuma* off Penang on 11 January 1944 and the German submarine *UIT23* on 15 February 1944.

Tally Ho! in dry dock in Colombo showing the results of her encounter with a Japanese 'Hyabusa' class escort on 24 February 1944. The Japanese vessel caught *Tally-Ho!* on the surface charging her batteries in the Malacca Strait and turned in to ram. Instead, the escort tore along the submarine's port side, her propeller gouging lumps from the submarine's saddle tanks with her screw. 'Just like a ruddy toastrack,' was one observer's perceptive comment on *Tally-Ho!*'s appearance.

HMS *Tantalus* which, under the command of Lieutenant Commander Hugh 'Rufus' Mackenzie, carried out the longest patrol by a British submarine during the Second World War. This lasted for fifty-five days from 3 January to 26 February 1945 in which *Tantalus* covered 11,692 miles. When *Tantalus* returned to Freemantle she had less than 5 per cent of her fuel remaining.

HMS *Terrapin* which was badly damaged during a Japanese depth-charge attack on 19 May 1945 when the submarine was in 57 ft of water. In a five-hour ordeal *Terrapin* suffered major damage; the explosion of one depth-charge 'dished in' the hull to a depth of 4 ft at one place on the port bow. *Terrapin* managed to surface and make her escape, but faced a long and dangerous journey back to Freemantle since she was unable to dive. However, help appeared in the shape of the US submarine *Cavalla* (Lieutenant Commander E.J. Kossler USN) who announced that she would escort *Terrapin* home. Kossler's announcement that 'in the event of enemy contact we will remain on the surface, we will not dive', is still remembered with gratitude by *Terrapin*'s crew.

The Japanese cruiser *Asigara* seen at Spithead for the 1937 Coronation Naval Review. On 8 June 1945 this vessel was torpedoed by HMS *Trenchant* (Commander A.R. Hezlet RN) at the northern end of the Banka Strait. In a perfectly executed attack, Hezlet had the cruiser trapped between the shore and a minefield and he hit her with five Mk VIII** torpedoes. After some thirty members of *Trenchant*'s crew had observed the sinking cruiser through the periscope, Hezlet fired another two torpedoes. Eventually *Asigara* capsized in great clouds of steam and smoke.

With the end of hostilities, the 'T' class construction programme was stopped. Two boats still under construction in Portsmouth Dockyard, *Thor* and *Tiara* are shown lying alongside the repair ship *Ranpura* in a very early stage of fitting out. The casing is complete only over the bows and the outboard boat has no plating over her saddle tanks. Both boats were subsequently broken up incomplete.

NMM N23502

HMS *Ursula*, one of three 'U' class boats designed before the war as training submarines to replace the ageing 'H' class. As designed they were unarmed, but six torpedo tubes were added. All six were forward facing with two external and four internal. Thus on a displacement of only 630/730 tons, the Us carried a very powerful armament. In this photograph *Ursula*'s two external tubes are clearly visible. *Ursula* served in both home waters and the Mediterranean.

Undine was the second of the three Group 1 'U' class submarines to be lost. She was depth-charged by the German 1st Minesweeping Flotilla on 7 January 1940. Unusually, all her ship's company survived and became prisoners of war. This photograph shows Able Seaman G. Campbell (centre) of her ship's company distributing Red Cross parcels in Oflag XIH. *Undine*'s first lieutenant, Lieutenant M. Harvey, became one of the famous 'Ghosts' in the PoW camp at Colditz.

An emotional reunion for some of *Ursula*'s crew with their relatives on the quayside at Blyth in 1939. Wives and girlfriends would often stay close to a submarine base and soon became familiar with the submarines' operating cycle. A late arrival was the cause of much anxiety. In many cases relatives' worst fears would be confirmed by the arrival of a telegram from the Admiralty.

HMS *Una* at Malta on 13 February 1943. *Una* and *Umpire* were built by the Royal Dockyard at Chatham whereas all the remaining forty boats were built at Barrow by Vickers. Note the shape of the bow compared to *Ursula*. The large lump on the bow made by the two external torpedo tubes provoked a number of complaints, namely that it reduced speed and caused a noticeable wave on the surface when the boat was running at periscope depth. As a result the two external tubes were removed and the bow lengthened and flattened. However, *Upholder, Unique, Upright, Usk, Utmost* and *Unbeaten* were too far advanced in their construction to be thus modified. As a result they retained the raised bow but were not fitted with external torpedo tubes. *Una* enjoyed a varied career in the Mediterranean (see Eric Newby's *Love and War in the Appenines* for a description of one operation in which she was involved) and then returned to the UK where she was employed in a training role.

Two famous 'U' class submarines alongside at Malta in 1942. The inboard boat is **HMS** *Urge*, commanded by Lieutenant E.P. Tomkinson. The outboard boat is *Upholder*, commanded by Lieutenant M.D. Wanklyn. This photograph shows the difference in the bow shape between the 'as-designed' *Upholder* and the modified *Urge*. Both these submarines were subsequently sunk in the Mediterranean, a campaign in which thirteen 'U' class boats were lost.

Lieutenant Commander M.D. Wanklyn (centre), CO of HMS *Upholder*, with some of his ship's company at Malta. After an inauspicious start (at one stage it was considered that he should be relieved of command), he quickly made his mark: his total score was over 100,000 tons of enemy shipping, the Italian destroyer *Libeccio* and the submarines *Tricheco* and *Ammiraglio St Bon*. He was awarded the Victoria Cross for a determined and skilfully executed attack on the Italian liner *Conte Rosso* on 24 May 1941. *Upholder* was sunk on 14 April 1942 on her last Mediterranean patrol, north-west of Tripoli after a savage depth-charge attack by the Italian destroyer *Pegaso*. There were no survivors. The Admiralty marked her loss by issuing a communiqué which concluded: 'The ship and her company are gone but the example and the inspiration remain.'

Lieutenant E.P. Tomkinson, commanding officer of *Urge*, with his wife at the launch of HM Submarine *P.31*, subsequently named *Uproar*. *Urge* was every bit as successful as *Upholder* although she did not receive the same recognition. *Urge* was lost with all her crew in late April 1942, probably as a result of a mine.

HMS *Unbroken* returns to Portsmouth on 26 April 1943 after a very successful deployment to the Mediterranean. *Unbroken* was the first submarine to operate from Malta following the return of submarines to the island in the summer of 1942. *Unbroken* carried out a number of operations including one special operation. She blocked the main west coast railway line on the Italian mainland for 24 hours for the expenditure of ten rounds of ammunition and survived a counter-attack which badly damaged the submarine's battery and led her to return to Malta with her crew wearing respirators on account of chlorine gas. When the battery was examined it was found that the Bakelite cells were so badly shattered that they had to be shovelled out of the boat.

Lieutenant Lynch Maydon at the periscope of HMS *Umbra*. On 15 June 1942, *Umbra* attacked the Italian battlefleet which was out to attack a westbound convoy heading for Malta. Maydon was aiming for the battleship *Littorio* and was about to fire when RAF aircraft began an attack on the Italian ships causing them to put their helms hard over. Maydon fired at long range and scored one hit on the *Littorio*. While observing the result of his handiwork he noticed that the cruiser *Trento* had stopped because of bomb damage and, after hurriedly reloading his torpedo tubes, finished her off.

The bridge of *Upstart* taken from the forward casing when at sea off Gibraltar. There was no separate gun tower hatch in the 'U' class and the gun's crew had to climb down the rungs on the port side of the conning tower to reach the gun. The gun crew had to be very nimble as they had to follow the same route back if their submarine had to dive in a hurry. The ammunition for the gun also came up the conning tower and was passed to the gun via a chute, the lower end of which can be seen to right of the gun barrel.

Upstart carried out her last patrol in the Aegean in September 1944 and found no targets. She was then ordered to land her eight torpedoes at Khíos in the Greek Islands to form a reserve for other submarines operating in the area. The task was not straightforward. Landing the torpedoes was difficult enough, but it was almost impossible to find any suitable means of transport to take the torpedoes from the quayside to the jetty. A mule cart proved unsuitable and it was only when the Chief ERA found a trolley in the local fire station that the task could be completed. Even so, the task occupied the whole of *Upstart*'s torpedo department together with a few locals and their mules. On 6 October 1944 *Untiring* called at Khíos and loaded four of these torpedoes.

The motor room of *Unruffled* showing the switchboard controls for the two electric motors on either side of the passageway. The main motors were located beneath the deck. The 'U' class had a diesel-electric power plant, unique in British submarine practice. Two Paxman Ricardo 615 b.h.p. diesels were directly connected to two generators which supplied power to the two 825 h.p. motors.

An unusual photograph taken by the Royal Canadian Navy showing *Unseen* diving in the Bay of Fundy in 1944 where she was operating as a training submarine. The camera was specially mounted for the task and the photograph shows the front of the bridge already underwater, and the top of the periscope standard, housing the search periscope, is about to go under.

A good photograph of *Usurper*'s bridge seen from the side of a depot ship. At the right of the picture is the bridge steering-wheel, behind which can be seen the covered head of the search periscope, inside the standard. On either side of the bridge, roughly level with the search periscope, are the two torpedo night sights. Behind the search periscope is the conning tower hatch. The engine room telegraphs are mounted on the after periscope standard (partially hidden by the ensign) and behind that at the rear of the bridge is the mast and aerial for the Type 291W air warning radar set. The X-shaped aerial had to be lowered with the dipoles facing fore and aft; failure to do this would result in the aerial being wrecked. The oval shape on the deck on the starboard side of the bridge is the upper end of the ammunition supply chute.

Lieutenant J.C.Y. Roxburgh and some of *United*'s ship's company on their return to Britain in October 1943. Each solid white bar on the Jolly Roger represents a merchant ship sunk, each broken white bar represents a merchant ship damaged. The broken red bar represents a damaged warship, while the U at the top left corner refers to the sinking of the Italian submarine *Remo* on 15 July 1943. Other symbols include three stars for successful gun actions, two daggers for special operations carried out and an egg-timer marking a thirty-six hour dive while *United* was hunted by Axis ASW forces.

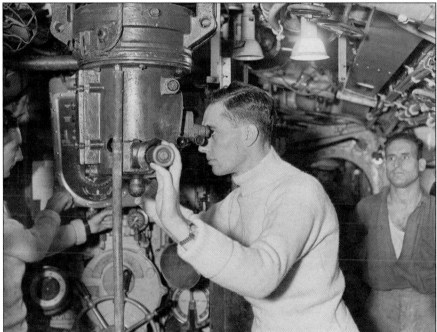

Lieutenant J.C.Y. Roxburgh at *United*'s periscope. Roxburgh went on to command a 'T' class submarine *Tapir* and sink *U486* in Norwegian waters just before the German surrender. At the time this photograph was taken, Roxburgh was the youngest submarine commander in the Royal Navy. He enjoyed a distinguished career in the post-war Navy and retired as Vice Admiral Sir John Roxburgh KCB DSO DSC. On the left is Sub Lieutenant P.G. Evatt RANVR, the 'Third Hand', working the 'Fruit Machine' (see page 106) while behind Roxburgh stands the telegraphist ready to read off the Director Angle from the periscope.

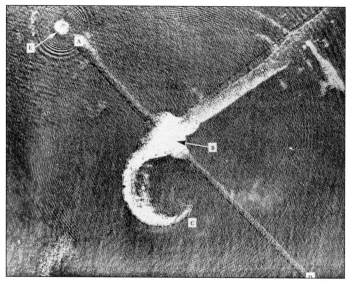

A remarkable photograph showing the after-effects of *United*'s attack on the 5,135 g.r.t. *Ringulv* on 14 June 1943. Four torpedoes were fired from 800 yd, two of which hit the target causing it to sink. The action was photographed by an RAF PRU Spitfire based at Malta. The line A–B is the track of the four torpedoes with B marking the explosion. The line B–D is the track of the two torpedoes which missed. The letter C shows the target which has wheeled round to port and is about to sink and E shows the explosion of a bomb dropped on *United* by an Axis aircraft.

HMS *Venturer*, seen here in Holy Loch on 28 August 1942, distinguished herself by sinking two German U-boats. The first was *U771* on 11 November 1944 and the second, *U864*, on 9 February 1945. The sinking of the latter was unique in submarine history since both boats were submerged at the time of the attack. *Venturer* detected the U-boat on her ASDIC and developed a good plot by using the Type 129 ASDIC in passive mode – to transmit a 'ping' would have given the game away. What *Venturer*'s commanding officer, Lieutenant J.S. Launders, later described as 'the most shameful periscope drill' on the part of the U-boat, gave him two good sightings of the German's periscope. When Launders judged the moment right, he fired four Mk VIII** torpedoes down the bearing and was rewarded with one hit. When *Venturer* surfaced Launders found oil, wooden wreckage and a large metal cylinder, later identified as the container for the Focke-Achegelis FA-330 autogyro: all that remained of *U864*.

HMS *Vulpine* under way in Liverpool Bay on 13 October 1944 with a schnorkel unit in place of her search periscope. The schnorkel was, in fact a dummy, the only purpose of which was to train RAF aircrew in spotting German U-boats equipped with the genuine article.

Three 'V' class boats (left to right: *Virtue*, *Vox(ii)* and *Voracious*) alongside the two 'T' class submarines (left to right: *Totem* and *Taurus*) at Sydney in the summer of 1945. Five 'V' class went out to the Mediterranean and then to the Far East where they were nominally required for ASW training. Even so, *Vigorous* carried out one patrol in the Malacca Strait in July 1945. Conditions in these small submarines, without any kind of air conditioning in the heat and humidity of the Far East, must have pushed the crew to the limits of their endurance.

No survey of British submarines in the Second World War would be complete without mention of the X-Craft midget submarines. These were four-man craft, armed with side charges each consisting of two tons of explosive. Alternatively a cargo of limpet mines could be carried. Undoubtedly their most famous feat was the attack on the *Tirpitz* in September 1943 but they also undertook covert reconnaissance of enemy coastlines, together with cable-cutting operations in the Far East. This photograph shows *X.24* flying a Jolly Roger to mark her return from an operation against a floating dock in Bergen. For the attack on the *Tirpitz* and the subsequent attack on the Japanese cruiser *Takao* in Singapore Harbour, no fewer than four VCs were awarded to X-Craft personnel.

THE ADMIRALTY
REGRETS

Since the Royal Navy's first submarine accident, controversy has arisen over the whole range of submarine operations and this has been stimulated whenever there has been a disaster in time of peace. Accidents were inevitable given the very nature of the craft and risks had to be taken if training for war was to be realistic.

Opinions varied in the Service on the relative merits of escaping from a submarine or waiting for the authorities to arrange salvage and lift the boat. Salvage was the preferred option until the Admiralty announced a change in policy in 1934. Henceforth submariners would not wait for rescue but would attempt to escape immediately, using specially designed breathing sets, the Davis Submarine Escape Apparatus (DSEA). From this beginning progress was slow but inexorable. The first officially sanctioned method was the Compartment Escape, a mass escape from a compartment flooded up to equalize pressure with the sea outside. Further developments led to the introduction of two-man escape chambers which could be flooded up very quickly, thus reducing the risks of oxygen poisoning. Developments were put on hold during the Second World War when many submarines had their escape hatches

secured to prevent them lifting if the boat were depth charged. Nevertheless by the end of the Second World War, a committee under the chairmanship of Rear Admiral Philip Ruck-Keene amassed a formidable amount of data on submarine escape, largely based on the evidence of successful escapes made during the Second World War. The Ruck-Keene Report was a most influential document and its provisions form the basis of escape policy today. Sadly financial stringency prevented most of Ruck-Keene's recommendations being implemented immediately. It took the loss of over sixty lives in the HMS *Truculent* disaster to spur the government into implementing the report's recommendations.

The introduction of nuclear-powered submarines meant that escape procedures had to adapt. Traditional methods of escape became impossible to use. The introduction of the Deep Submergence Rescue Vehicle means that a submarine's crew trapped in extremely deep water can be transferred to another submarine without even getting wet! The development of escape procedures in the Royal Navy has been a remarkable collaboration between submariners, engineers and the medical profession. It is to be hoped that the results of their work are never again put to the test.

The funeral procession for the crew of *A.1* nearing Haslar cemetery in Gosport. *A.1* was the first British submarine to be sunk as a result of an accident in peacetime. On 18 March 1904 she was struck by the liner *Berwick Castle* while submerged, with the loss of all eleven members of her crew. This type of occasion was conducted with much ceremony, led by bands with the route lined with spectators and mourners. The one mile road between the main gate of the RN hospital at Haslar and Haslar Cemetery was thus known as 'Dead Man's Mile'.

Two submariners demonstrating the Rees-Hall escape apparatus – the first submarine escape apparatus in use in the Royal Navy. It consisted of a hard helmet and a belted long-sleeved tunic. Inside the tunic was a canister of sodium peroxide which gave off oxygen while absorbing carbon dioxide. The use of sodium peroxide was an interesting choice as it had a tendency to burst into flames if it became wet! The equipment was very bulky and doubts existed about the wearer's ability to exit through the upper hatch of a submarine.

The crew of a 'C' class submarine wearing their Rees-Hall suits. The 'C' class boats were the first to be fitted with lockers for stowing the gear, and air locks but there was barely room for the crew and essential stores, let alone all this equipment. Moreover, since there were no internal bulkheads in the Cs, flooding-up the boat to facilitate an escape would have been a lengthy and dangerous process. There is no record of the Rees-Hall apparatus ever being used.

A pre-war view of *C.16* under way in Haslar Creek. On 16 April 1917 the submarine was lost following a collision with the destroyer HMS *Melampus* off Harwich. Although her conning tower was damaged in the collision and the lower hatch was leaking, the hull was basically sound. The commanding officer, Lieutenant Harold Boase RN, ordered main ballast blown but this action only succeeded in raising the bow to within 16 ft of the surface. After the submarine had been raised it was found that the air line bringing HP air to the whistle was broken and the stopcock had been left open. Air from the groups was thus simply blown into the sea. The First Lieutenant, Mr Samuel Anderson, then tried to escape via one of the torpedo tubes and take a note to rescuers on the surface. Anderson crammed his way into the 18 inch diameter tube with a note tied to his wrist which read: 'We are in 16ft of water. The way out is to lift the bows by the spectacle and haul us out of the boat by the tubes.' The attempt failed either because Anderson was too big and was unable to get out of the tube or because the submarine's angle of inclination was too great.

C.16 after being raised following the collision with *Melampus*. The photograph shows damage to the conning tower. After the failure of Anderson's escape the fifteen survivors gathered beneath the forward hatch wearing lifejackets. They flooded up the interior of the submarine and then tried to open the forward hatch. The hatch would not open fully and when it was dropped, a pig of lead attached to a fender swung under the joint and held the lid open by a gap of 2 inches. The air lock in the boat was lost and the survivors drowned. *C.16* was subsequently sold for scrap and the officers and men of her ship's company buried at Harwich. Among the possessions of Able Seaman Alfred Humpreys was a letter to his family: 'From Stan to Mother, Father, May and all Friends. Best of luck to all. Thought of you till last moment. Let my girl know at 60, Cuthbert St. Was rammed by destroyer or something at 10.30am. Writing this seven hours after given up all hope.'

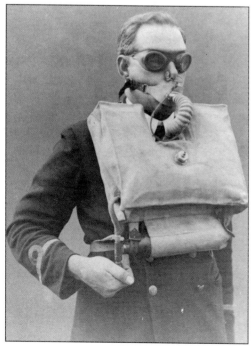

Commissioned Gunner Lacey demonstrating the Davis Submarine Escape Apparatus (DSEA) which was to serve the Navy in a variety of roles from its adoption in 1929 until the late 1950s. The wearer breathed oxygen which was supplied from an HP cylinder from the breathing bag worn on the chest. He exhaled carbon dioxide which was diverted through a valve in the mouthpiece into a second cylinder, containing a purifying agent, before being returned to the breathing bag. Each set came complete with goggles, a nose clip and an apron, and the breathing bag was fitted with an apron or drogue to prevent the wearer ascending too fast.

Escape training using the DSEA set from a 15-ft tank in HMS *Dolphin*. The trainee is just beginning his ascent to the surface. The artificiality of such training is apparent. DSEA was first used when the submarine *Poseidon* was rammed and sunk by the Chinese steamer *Yuta*. Eight men were trapped in the fore ends and eighteen at the after end of the boat. None of those from the after end escaped but six of those from the fore ends, led by Petty Officer Willis, reached the surface.

The after chamber in *Tribune*. Circular quick-acting doors allowed access from either side although a separate bulkhead door was fitted, allowing the chamber to be bypassed. Two sets of controls were fitted so that the chamber could be worked from whichever side remained unflooded. Each chamber could accomodate two men. The escape procedure was simple: two men would enter the compartment wearing their DSEA sets and close the doors behind them. They would then release the clips on the upper hatch so that the hatch was held down by sea pressure and an external toe clip. Sea water was then admitted through a flood valve and the air was vented outboard. Once the chamber was flooded the external toe clip was released, the men pushed up the upper hatch and swam up to the surface. Those inside the submarine could watch proceedings through special glass ports. When the chamber was empty they could shut the upper lid and drain the chamber down into the bilges. The next two men could then enter and the process would be repeated. These escape chambers were the most advanced escape equipment fitted in a British submarine until the introduction of the one-man chambers fitted in the 'Porpoise' and 'Oberon' class boats built in the 1950s and 60s.

The stern of HMS *Thetis* rises above the waters of Liverpool Bay after the submarine sunk during her first dive on 1 June 1939. The submarine sank because the rear door to No. 5 torpedo tube had been opened while the bow cap was open. For various reasons it was not possible to tell before opening the rear door whether the tube was flooded or not. It proved impossible to contain the inrush of water and the submarine sank to the bottom. The crew succeeded in raising the stern of the submarine throughout the night of 1/2 June, so that when she was found at dawn on 2 June by the destroyer *Brazen*, some eighteen feet of her stern were above the water.

Despite the fact that the after-escape chamber was less than 20 ft from the surface, only four men succeeded in escaping from *Thetis*: Captain H.P. Oram, the captain of *S.5*, the flotilla which *Thetis* was scheduled to join; Lieutenant Frederick Woods, the submarine's torpedo officer; Leading Stoker Walter Arnold (seen here, left, with his brothers) and Frank Shaw, a Cammell Laird fitter. After Arnold and Shaw escaped, the seamen operating the chamber, by now suffering the lethal effects of carbon dioxide poisoning, made an error in the drill for working the chamber so that the upper hatch could not be opened. Another four men tried to use the chamber but were dragged out dead or dying having failed to open the upper hatch.

The salvage vessel *Vigilant* closes *Thetis'* stern in a last desperate effort to free those trapped inside the submarine. Moments after this photograph was taken *Thetis* slipped beneath the waves for the last time.

Author's Collection

A memorial postcard produced following the *Thetis* accident. Stoker Arnold's name appears erroneously in the second column, fourth from the top. At the time of her loss 103 of the crew were onboard. In addition to *Thetis'* complement of 53 men, there were an additional 50 passengers, most of whom were directly concerned with the trials. This included 26 employees of Cammell Laird, the builder; 9 other naval officers; 4 employees of Vickers Armstrong; 1 from Brown Bros and 2 from Liverpool City caterers who provided the 'big-eats' that were such a feature of the occasion. At the last minute the Mersey River Pilot, who had supervised *Thetis'* passage down the Mersey, was asked if he wanted to remain onboard for the dive and he accepted.

Author's Collection

Chief ERA George Killen (right) who supervised the escape of 20 men from the engine room of HMS *Umpire* after she had been rammed and sunk by the trawler *Peter Hendricks* on 19 July 1941. After ensuring that all were wearing their DSEA sets Killen left the submarine and, in his own words, 'walked around on the casing a bit' to check that the way up was not fouled, before re-entering the submarine to supervise the escape. He was the last to leave. He was rewarded with a BEM, though many believe he deserved a higher honour. The unidentified individual on the left shows what the well-dressed ERA messman wears at sea!

Gus Britton

The shattered hull of HMS *Truculent* raised after her loss on 12 January 1950 following a collision with the Swedish tanker *Divina* in the Thames Estuary. A total of 64 men made successful escapes from the engine room and after ends. Yet only 10 survived – the remainder perished from hypothermia as they were carried out to sea on an ebbing tide. Four years earlier the Ruck-Keene escape committee had recommended the provision of immersion suits that would protect a man on the surface following an escape. The recommendation had not been carried through on the grounds of expense – such was the price of austerity.

HMS *Affray* diving – a photograph taken in the late 1940s. On 16 April 1951 she sailed for an exercise in the English Channel carrying a total of 75 officers and men. In addition to her own ship's company, some of whom were landed to make way for the extras, she was carrying a Submarine Officers Training Class of 23 and a party of Royal Marine Commandos. Her last signal was made at 21.00 that evening and when by the next morning the routine signal had not been received, the SUBSUNK procedure was put into effect. Regretfully by the evening of 19 April when nothing had been found, the search was called off as there could be no hope of anyone remaining alive inside the submarine.

The diving ship *Reclaim* hauls up *Affray's* schnorckel mast on 1 July 1951. The mast had broken off at the base and subsequent examination revealed that there was a structural weakness in that area. However there was no evidence to suggest whether the mast had broken as a result of a collision or as the result of an internal battery explosion. The efforts of the salvors then centred on checking whether the snort mast hull-induction valve was shut, thus sealing off any ingress of water following the break of the snort mast. After a portion of the casing was ripped off, X-ray photography using radioactive isotopes was used. However these operations were abruptly suspended when a diver dropped an isotope beside *Affray* which could not be recovered. It was considered unsafe for divers to remain in the area of the wreck and the operation was abandoned.

S.–463c.   (Revised May, 1942)   Register No...................

N.B.—This account is to be rendered for a period of 12 months *from the date of taking charge*, and for each ensuing 12 months from the date of completing the last Account, or for any shorter period on being superseded or invalided, or on the Destroyer, &c., being paid off, as required by Article 1372 of the King's Regulations and Admiralty Instructions.

FOR DESTROYERS, SUBMARINES, &c., CARRYING No. 4, No. 5 or No. 6 UNITS OF MEDICAL STORES.

AN ACCOUNT of the Receipts and Issues, &c., of MEDICINES and MEDICAL STORES

on board His Majesty's *Submarine "AFFRAY"* .... Accounting Officer
SURGEON COMMANDER

Between   30ᵗʰ March   19 51   (1) S.M. *Recommissioned*

19ᵗʰ April   19 51   (2) *"Lost at Sea"*

(1) Here insert "Commissioned"; "Survey from......................"; or "Continued by Survey".
(2) Here insert "Paid Off"; "Survey to......................"; or "Continues by Survey".

Average Complement during the period of this Account, No............ 75

To: *Approved and Transmitted,*
Medical Director-General of the Navy,
Admiralty, ...Captain or Commanding Officer
London, S.W.1.   Date....................

M.D. Sta. 10154/42.

S.463c.

A last poignant note – the closing of HMS *Affray*'s accounts.

The 100 ft Submarine Escape Training Tower (SETT) at HMS *Dolphin*. All submariners undergo escape training as part of their initiation and then at regular intervals throughout their careers. The tower is equipped with an escape tank at the bottom from which escapes are conducted under tightly-controlled conditions. During a free ascent the escapee has to exhale vigorously to relieve air pressure in the lungs – the instructors remind those not breathing out hard enough to do so with a swift jab in the midriff!

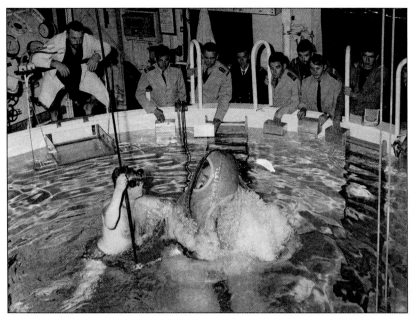

Lieutenant Commander Matthew Todd examining a trainee wearing an immersion suit following an escape at the upper end of the tank in 1968. The session is being witnessed by officers of the French Navy who subsequently adopted the system for their 'Le Redoubtable' class SSBNs. Wearing such an immersion suit it is possible for escapes to be conducted from depths of 600 feet; that is anywhere on the continental shelf where a submarine is most at risk from collision with other maritime craft. The suit is constantly being updated with the latest version, the Mk 10, containing an integrated lifeboat and homing beacon.

A trainee reaches the surface in dramatic fashion wearing a Mk 6 suit in 1975. The suit protected the wearer from hypothermia when on the surface, and had such suits been provided for the crew of *Truculent*, then many more lives would have been saved. However this means of escape is only practicable down to a certain depth which is well exceeded by modern deep-diving SSNs. An alternative method of escape had to be developed for survivors of a submarine sunk in very deep water off the continental shelf which resulted in the development of the Deep Submergence Rescue Vessel (DSRV).

The United States developed the DSRV and maintain one on each coast which could be despatched to the site of a submarine accident in an emergency. It is a mini submarine which can attach itself to the escape hatch of a stricken vessel and carry 20 survivors at a time. Here the DSRV *Avalon* arrives at Prestwick airport and is seen emerging from the hold of a USAF C-5 Galaxy transport aircraft.

HMS *Victorious*, one of the Royal Navy's new 'Trident' class SSBNs with the DSRV *Avalon* embarked. *Avalon*'s escape skirt, which attaches to the victim submarine's escape tower forming a watertight seal, can be clearly seen below the craft. *Avalon*'s skirt is compatible with the escape towers fitted to US, British, French and Russian nuclear submarines.

INTO
THE NUCLEAR AGE
1945-1954

The most immediate postwar priority was the reduction in the size of the submarine fleet to a more appropriate level and the release of the 'hostilities only' officers and ratings back to their civilian occupations. Although the cuts in submarine numbers were severe, they were not as drastic as those implemented throughout the rest of the fleet, and by the mid-1950s the submarine force made up a greater percentage of the Royal Navy's order of battle than ever before.

This was just as well, since the main threat facing the Royal Navy in the postwar period was the rapidly expanding Soviet submarine fleet, built with the aid of 'liberated' German technology. The realities of Britain's economic situation meant that the maintenance of a large surface force to counter the threat was out of the question, so in 1948 the interception and destruction of enemy submarines was designated as the 'primary operational function' of the British submarine fleet. At that moment the Service ceased to be a 'private navy' within the Royal Navy, but instead took its place at the forefront of British naval planning.

Clearly a new type of submarine was needed but until the necessary research and development required for a new boat could be completed – which included experimenting with High Test Peroxide as a fuel – some form of stopgap was needed. The result was the conversion of some 'T' class boats and nearly all the 'A' class to give them a streamlined form and faster underwater speed. This greatly enhanced their performance although it must be said that the development of sensors and weapons during this period did not keep pace with advances in design and construction.

In order to look at high speed, long endurance options and following on from the experience gained from the captured U-1407 (HMS *Meteorite*) the Royal Navy built two unarmed submarines fitted with improved high test peroxide (HTP) engines, HMS *Explorer* and *Excalibur*, (colloquially known as the 'exploder' class). By the time they were commissioned in 1958, spectacular success had been achieved by the US Navy with nuclear power, so the experiment was discontinued.

The first new British postwar design of a diesel-electric submarine was the 'Porpoise' class, and eight were laid down between 1955–58. This successful class was soon followed by the Oberons, of which thirteen were built between 1957 and 1962. These large patrol submarines, which were capable of remaining dived for several weeks, could operate in any part of the world, and were extremely quiet, a feature which when combined with their excellent sensor fit made them highly capable conventional submarines.

They were designated SSK (submarine submerged killer), a reflection of the 'primary operational function' specified in 1948. By the mid-70s the Soviet submarine arm had grown to over 400 hulls, 100 of them being nuclear powered. The Soviet threat had also grown through a shift in strategy as well as an increase in numbers and the time-honoured notion of the Soviet Navy being a purely defensive force was abandoned, in favour of that of carrying the battle to the enemy, with the submarine being the tip of the spear that could strike at the West's Aircraft Carrier Battle Groups, its deterrent missile submarines, and its sea lines of communications. A great deal of the working lives of the 'O's and 'P's was thus spent on anti-submarine operations, often working with maritime patrol aircraft of the Royal Air Force, in areas where the allies enjoyed air superiority, but more often operating independently far from home.

While the Royal Navy was building up its fleet of nuclear-powered submarines at the rate of one every fifteen months during the late 1960s and 1970s, its SSKs skilfully bore the brunt of the global panoply of submarine operations. Offensive and defensive anti-submarine and anti-ship operations; forward surveillance; special forces operations; training surface and air forces; weapon development and, last but not least, showing the flag, were all tasks undertaken with great success over a period of more than thirty years.

Yet for all their excellence, the Porpoises and Oberons, and their replacement 'Upholder' class, could never overcome the limitations imposed by their slow speed of deployment which, allied to the lack of forward support bases, ruled them out from the front line of rapid response in a world scenario dominated increasingly by brush fire confrontations.

Sadly, as a dividend of peace, the era of the conventional submarine, after ninety-three years of wonderful service in the Royal Navy, drew to a close in 1994.

HMS *Thrasher* returns to Portsmouth in October 1945 following her third commission in the Far East. *Thrasher* was one of only a few British submarines to serve in all three theatres of operations.

Wright & Logan

HMS *Trident*, another famous 'T' class submarine, awaiting breaking up at Newport. The end of hostilities marked a drastic reduction in the number of submarines in commission. All the riveted 'S' and 'T' class boats, together with the Us and Vs were scheduled for disposal together with the surviving Rivers and minelayers.

Author's Collection

Some submarines were expended in trials to determine the strength of their construction. This photograph shows the remains of *Stoic*, a riveted 'S' class submarine, in May 1949 after she had been lowered from lifting craft and dropped to a depth at which her pressure hull collapsed. In *Stoic*'s case the collapse came when she reached 532 ft and the hull gave way in the area of the forward torpedo loading hatch. A similar test in June 1949 with a welded S-boat, *Supreme*, saw the boat reach 647 ft before collapsing.

HMS *Amphion* was the first of sixteen 'A' class submarines, the only class to be designed during the Second World War. The As were intended for operations in the Far East and so had a high surface speed, 18.5 knots, considerable endurance (10,500 miles at 11 knots) and enhanced habitability. Armament consisted of six bow tubes and four stern tubes. A 4 inch Mk XXIII gun and 20 mm Oerlikon completed the armament. *Amphion* is shown as completed with a low bow. Sea keeping problems later caused this bow to be raised by the addition of a bow buoyancy tank.

HMS *Seraph* after her conversion to a high-speed target submarine. The conversion actually took place in 1944 and was intended to fit her for use as a high-speed target for ASW forces in training, to counter the threat posed by the German Type XXI. The gun and all external fittings were removed from the casing, her engines and motors were upgraded, a high capacity battery fitted and she was given 'T' class propellers which had coarser pitch. The result was an increase in her underwater speed from 9 to 12 knots. *Sceptre, Satyr* and *Statesman* of the 1941 programme and *Selene, Solent* and *Sleuth* of the 1942/3 programme were similarly converted. The use of these craft provided much useful data and pointed the way forward to the modern nuclear submarine.

HMS *Tradewind*, a Group 3 T-boat, after her conversion to an acoustic trials submarine. All her armamnet was removed or blanked off with the exception of two torpedo tubes and she was given a reduced and faired bridge structure. Her British ASDIC suite was removed and replaced by a German BALKON passive hydrophone in the keel and a NIEBLUNG transducer in a fairing, forward of the conning tower.

Wright & Logan

One of the most important developments in the post-war period was the introduction of the Schnorckel – a tube that allowed the submarine to take air into the boat when dived and thus run her diesel engines. First fitted in *Truant* in 1945 it was eventually universally fitted, although the weight of the mast meant that submarines had to dispense with their 4 inch guns. This photograph shows the mast being erected in *Trespasser*.

Author's Collection

HMS *Truncheon* after her ad hoc refit in 1951 by the staff of the depot ship HMS *Montclare*. Her bow external torpedo tubes and gun were removed, the conning tower faired and she was fitted with an American JT hydrophone on the forward casing. These modifications were to prepare her for the Royal Navy's first formal submarine vs. submarine exercises in which she played the part of the 'defender' against HMS *Alcide*. While the trials showed some promise they, together with further exercises with *Tireless* and *Tally-Ho!*, prompted Flag Officer Submarines to comment that, 'the present general purpose submarine . . . is unlikely to be very successful in the A/S role'.

Wright & Logan

HMS *Taciturn* was the first of eight 'T' conversions in which the hull was lengthened by 14 ft (12 ft in *Thermopylae*, *Turpin* and *Totem*, 20 ft in *Tabard*, *Tiptoe*, *Trump* and *Truncheon*) to incorporate an extra battery and a second pair of motors. At the same time all external fittings on the casing were removed to give a streamlined form and the periscopes and masts above the bridge enclosed in a 'fin'. A small bridge was fitted at the forward end of the fin. This was very low and gave no end of problems which one CO described as 'an abortion of a bridge'.

Author's Collection

HMS *Tabard* one of the four 'Super Ts' which were lengthened by 20 ft. Note the different bridge configuration in which the bridge was incorporated as part of the fin. The conversion considerably enhanced these submarines' performance. *Totem* recorded dived speeds in excess of 18 knots and her commanding officer described A/S exercises as 'money for old rope'.

Author's Collection

HMS *Tireless* was one of five T-boats selected for 'streamlining', an economy conversion programme in which the hull and casing were streamlined and a new fin was fitted; no other structural modifications were carried out.

Author's Collection

The As underwent a similar conversion to the Ts although their hulls were not lengthened as in the 'T' conversions. This photograph shows *Acheron* passing under Brooklyn Bridge in New York harbour during a port visit in April 1966.

HMS *Aeneas* with the experimental Submarine Launched Airflight Missile (SLAM) system fitted to her fin. The system consisted of four Blowpipe missiles clustered around a TV camera on a telescopic mast and was designed to thin out prosecuting helicopters which were, and still are, considered a major threat because of their mobility and unpredictability in the close-screening role. The system was never introduced into the Service and when *Aeneas* paid off in 1972, some wag painted SS *Gilette* on her after casing – a realistic forecast of her fate.

HMS *Alliance*, flying her paying-off pennant, arrives at Portsmouth for the last time in 1973. In 1979 she was placed on blocks to become the centre piece of the Royal Navy Submarine Museum with openings cut into the pressure hull for easy access. She remains there today as a proud monument to the Submarine Service.

Another era came to an end with the paying off of HMS *Andrew* in 1974. She was the last submarine to carry the 4 inch gun that had served the Service so well. Her commanding officer marked the last firing in December 1974 with a signal to the Admiralty: 'The reek of cordite has passed from the Royal Navy's Submarine Service. Last gun action conducted at 03 1330Z. May the art of submarine gunnery rest in peace but never be forgotten.' *Andrew* is shown here alongside HMS *Belfast* in London on her final port visit before paying off.

In 1956 the Royal Navy commissioned two experimental submarines, HMS *Explorer* and HMS *Excalibur*. These two boats were propelled by High Test Peroxide (HTP), a curious substance which in its weakest form can be used to dye hair blond but, in its strongest manufactured form is capable of driving submarines, rockets and torpedoes. The propulsion design was based on the Walter Engine, used in later German U-boats, one of which, *U1407*, was captured in 1945 and commissioned as HMS *Meteorite*. The principle of HTP was that when it decomposed (which it did naturally) it gave off oxygen and superheated steam; these by-products, when burnt with kerosene, provided a rapid production of high pressure gases. These were used to propel turbines. This gave the submarine a very high underwater speed, albeit for short periods.

While the Royal Navy was experimenting with high-speed options, it also had one eye on the conventional future. So 1956 also saw the birth of a new class of conventional submarine, specifically designed to oppose other submarines. HMS *Porpoise* is seen here on the building slip at Vickers Shipbuilders, Barrow. Her machinery was acoustically dampened with flexible mountings, and she was fitted with the very latest in passive sonar, Type 187, which was capable of long-range detection of another snorting submarine. She had another sonar set Type 719, fitted in the keel; because of its high rotation it was excellent for clearing the immediate surface picture and helping to get the submarine to periscope depth safely. Eight of the class were built, all named after fish and sea mammals.

Navy News

Her Majesty revisiting HMS *Dolphin* for the presentation of the Submarine Service's second colour in 1990, the first having been presented by her in 1959. She is addressing Commander Tim Cannon, winner of the Queen's Gallantry Medal for controlling a major fire in the SSN HMS *Warspite*. In the background is Flag Officer Submarines, Rear Admiral Frank Grenier.

A 'Porpoise' class submarine rises eerily through the placid waters of the Gareloch in 1960. The Gareloch was deep enough to allow a quick post-maintenance period dive to check for leaks, particularly if work had been conducted on sensitive areas such as hull valves (which kept out the sea) or the snort system (that allowed you to draw air into the boat for the main engines).

The Submarine Depot Ship HMS *Adamant* with her fourteen submarines of the Second Submarine Squadron Flotilla in Falmouth Bay in August 1962. There is a motley mixture of classes in sight; S-boats, T-boats, A-boats with their flat ballast tanks, and P-boats with their gleaming Type 187 sonar domes. The depot ship provided accommodation, administration and stores support to her 'chicks', and was capable of deploying to any suitable harbour.

Navy News

HMS *Dolphin* in 1967 with her 'trots' (submarine berths) and her hands full! It was at Fort Blockhouse, hidden by the modern buildings, that the Submarine Service first found a home. Dispatched to the far side of Portsmouth Harbour in 1902 lest their frequent engine explosions besmirched the gleaming grey paint of the Dreadnoughts, generations of submarines found comfort in the bosom of their Alma Mater.

That wasn't supposed to happen! A practice torpedo dropped by a Sea King helicopter from the aircraft carrier HMS *Ark Royal*, instead of turning away in its final approach, kept going and embedded itself in the casing of HMS *Walrus*. An essential role of these submarines was to provide 'friendly' opposition in order to maintain and sharpen the skills of ASW surface and air forces in the face of growing Soviet submarine capability.

A 'Porpoise' class SSK making her way out of Portsmouth Harbour having just left her home base of HMS *Dolphin* in Gosport, Hampshire. In the background is Semaphore Tower, the offices of the former Flag Officer Portsmouth, but still the office of the Queen's Harbourmaster whose barge can be seen in the background. The masts of HMS *Victory*, still in commission and the flagship of the Second Sea Lord and Commander in Chief Naval Home Command, can be seen behind Semaphore Tower. The Gosport ferry, left, remains an important part of the maritime tapestry of the harbour.

HMS *Finwhale* on passage down the Johore Strait, Singapore, in 1970. Note the Oerlikon gun mounted forward of the fin. Although the Borneo conflict had ended a number of years earlier, the option of being fitted with the gun when serving in Far East waters remained. A number of COs

enthusiastically embraced the opportunity to revive submarine gunnery skills! The Royal Navy maintained a three-boat flotilla of submarines, based on the depot ship **HMS** *Forth* until 1973, the year that signalled their withdrawal from the east of Suez.

HMS *Orpheus* entering Portsmouth harbour for paying-off into refit in 1973, having just returned as the last submarine of the Seventh Submarine Squadron in Singapore.

Captain Bob Garson

HMS *Porpoise* on passage up the Gareloch towards the Clyde Submarine Base in 1978. In that year she was twenty-one years old, and the grand old lady of the submarine flotilla. She was the first of this highly successful class of conventionally powered submarines, which were the fore-runners of the 'Oberon' class. By the end of their working life this class had given excellent service world wide.

An 'Oberon' class, in the early morning light, on passage in an uncomfortable beam sea. It was in conditions like these, where the ship rolled considerably, that submariners would have quoted the famous adage 'happiness is 600 feet in a Force 10'! This class of conventional submarine of which thirteen were built, entered the Royal Navy in the late 1960s were undoubtedly the finest of their type in the world during their era, with the last, HMS *Opossum* paying-off in 1993. During the late 1980s they were given a new lease of life with the introduction of a new, highly automated sonar Type 2051, a salvo capability for firing the Tigerfish torpedo, and the capability to fire the Royal Navy Sub-Harpoon missile. They saw service all over the world, and were bought by Australia, Canada, Brazil and Chile.

HMS *Otter* sporting her new Type 2051 sonar dome, starting to get the casing ready for passage. Note the wire at the back of the submarine. This was the towing cable for her Towed Array sonar, a long-listening device deployed well clear of any submarine self-noise interference, which was capable of detecting low frequency noise (readily transmitted through the ocean) at very long range. As well as early warning reporting, the SSK often worked with RAF Nimrod Maritime Patrol Aircraft who would endeavour to localize the SSKs reported long-range contacts. It was an effective combination.

HMS *Dolphin*, in her final days as an operational submarine base, with a brood of 'Oberon' chicks alongside. The base was intended to continue to support the new 'Upholder' class of conventional submarine; however they fell victim to the 'peace dividend'.

Navy News

HMS *Opossum* sporting 'middle eastern' colours after Operation Desert Storm. The Commanding Officer had wanted to paint a set of teeth on the bow but his Captain SM thought that this was going too far. The picture of their world-wide capability is reinforced by the memory of HMS *Onyx*'s service during the Falklands War. The contributions made in intelligence gathering, Special Forces operations, anti-submarine and anti-ship warfare and training significantly reinforced the proud legacy of the Submarine Service.

Commander S. Upright

The modern 'Upholder' class conventional submarines were ordered to replace the 'Oberon' class in the late 1980s. At the time of the order the cold war was at its height, and the heady days of *détente* with Russia and the break-up of the Soviet Bloc was a pipedream. These submarines were designed to precise specifications and given the specific mission of filling the Greenland/Iceland/Faeroes/Shetland Gaps to the north of the UK and the back door from the Norwegian Sea to the Atlantic. They paid the price of not being established in other roles by the time of disguised defence reviews following the cold war, and no sooner had they entered service then they were being offered for sale to overseas nations. There is no question that if their sacrifice was made to protect our SSN numbers, then it was right to bring to an end the magnificent diesel era of the Service, and to rely on our allies for the essential elements of training against the growing threat of SSKs in the hands of potential enemies. Nevertheless, their departure caused much sadness, particularly because of their excellence and promise as a class. HMS *Unicorn* is seen here under a rain shower in Faslane.

Navy News

HMS *Ursula* at the D-Day review on 5 June 1994. It was so appropriate that an 'Upholder' class should represent the Royal Navy Submarine Service at these celebrations. Names such as Wanklyn (*Upholder*), Phillips (*Ursula*), Crawford (*Unseen*) bring memories of some of our Second World War heroes flooding back. *Resurgam* – we shall rise again – one of the mottoes of the Submarine Service is reinforced by the other: 'We come Unseen'.

Navy News

The final salute to conventional submarine warfare in the Royal Navy. All four *Upholders*, on their way to be put in mothballs in Barrow.

HMS *Neptune*

UNDERWAY ON NUCLEAR POWER

'Underway on nuclear power' is the now famous signal sent by the Commanding Officer of USS *Nautilus* on 17 January 1955 as she sailed from Groton, Connecticut. Her departure represented the culmination of a dream pursued relentlessly by Admiral Hyman G. Rickover USN, since his first involvement with the USA's nuclear propulsion programme in 1946. With the construction of USS *Nautilus*, the world was given its first true submarine, and with it came a revolution in the field of underwater warfare. With almost unlimited endurance (food for the crew being the limiting factor!), it married the submarine's traditional strengths of stealth and surprise with a speed greater than its potential quarry.

Admiral of the Fleet, Earl Mountbatten, First Sea Lord between 1955 and 1959, was one of the driving forces behind the Royal Navy's venture into nuclear power, seeing its introduction into submarines as essential if British sea power was not to wither on the vine. It was also his intervention in 1959, now as Chief of Defence Staff, that secured the provision of a complete Skipjack power plant from the United States to be fitted into HMS *Dreadnought* in order to keep her development on track as the British-designed reactor was not to be ready on time. The keel of HMS *Dreadnought* was laid in June 1959 by HRH The Duke of Edinburgh, and she was launched by Her Majesty the Queen on 21 October 1960. She finally commissioned in April 1963, and the greatest step forward in the history of British submarines had been taken since 1901, the year of the Service's birth.

It is not hard to see why the USA was enthusiastic to have its traditional ally join 'the nuclear propulsion' club, particularly given its strategic geographic location. With Admiral Gorshkov at the helm of the Soviet Navy, a post he was to hold for thirty years, it was pressing ahead with Stalin's plans to have 1,200 submarines in the Soviet Order of Battle. The year 1967 was profoundly important in that it saw the introduction of the 'Yankee' class SSBN, the 'Charlie' class SSGN (anti-ship missile firer) and the 'Victor' class SSN, all of which added immense power and flexibility to the Soviet submarine fleet since they represented a step change in technology. Soviet development did not stop there for in 1971, the titanium-hulled *Alfa* was produced, capable of 42 knots and a depth of 900 metres. The *Victor III*, the *Sierra*, and more recently, the *Akula* have followed, all formidable opponents by any standards. In anti-ship missile firing submarine development, the West has witnessed the introduction of the 'Oscar' class SSGN with its awesome load of aptly named 'Shipwreck' missiles.

In SSBN terms, the Soviet strategic missile-carrying submarines grow ever larger and their missile loads more potent and significantly longer in range. The *Delta IV* appeared in 1984, followed shortly by the largest submarine ever built, the *Typhoon*. This leviathan of the deep is in fact two Delta hulls joined together, is fitted with 20 missile tubes, and weighs in the order of 30,000 tons. This SSBN force is well known for operating in areas close to the Atlantic icecap in order to enhance their survivability.

The SSN remains the most potent force at sea that will assure the supremacy of western navies, which for maritime nations 'Doth the well-being of the state depend'. A continuing role will be the protection of the National Deterrent, described in 1968 as 'the best insurance policy the nation ever had'.

The development of the Polaris Missile programme began at the same time as *Nautilus* was launched in 1955, in the USA. The detonation of the first Soviet H-bomb caused the US Army and Navy to collaborate on the development of a sea-borne inter-continental strategic missile. It was recognized that the submarine was the ultimate in deterrent platforms because, unlike fixed land installations or aircraft, it was mobile, gave little warning and, providing that it was quiet, almost invulnerable. The result of this collaboration was the Jupiter missile. A Special Projects Office was established under Rear Admiral William Raborn who gathered together a team of experts, including a technical director, Captain Levering Smith, who in turn recruited the German missile expert, Wernher Von Braun. They were to convince the Navy Department that Jupiter was not suitable for naval use because of its liquid-fuel propellant and that a solid-fuel rocket should be developed. Thus the Polaris project was born on 1 January 1957.

The UK watched this progress with interest, though intent on basing its own deterrent on the airborne Skybolt, carried by a fleet of 'V' bombers, and the land-based Blue Streak missiles. When these projects were cancelled or failed, the fact that the Royal Navy was able to suggest a speedy and coherent alternative was once again due to the foresight of Admiral Mountbatten who, as First Sea Lord, had secured the agreement in 1958 of Admiral Arleigh Burke, the US Chief of Naval Operations, to allow the appointment of a British Liasion Officer to Raborn's Special Project team. When Skybolt foundered in the US in 1962, President Kennedy met with Prime Minister Harold

Macmillan in Nassau on 20–21 December of that year and agreed to transfer Polaris to Britain. The UK would develop and manufacture its own warheads, which would be under national control, thus making the deterrent independent. Four days later, the UK Polaris Executive was established and the Flag Officer Submarines, Rear Admiral Hugh 'Rufus' Mackenzie DSO* DSC, a distinguished Second World War Commanding Officer, was chosen to head it. With a target date of 1968, the team took on this massive project which called for much personal sacrifice and incredibly hard work. The fact that they succeeded is a stunning accolade to the individuals concerned and to British industry.

The history of Polaris, with 229 unbroken patrols, was a total success and, with its mid-life update of Chevaline in 1982, it remained a truly credible deterrent until HMS *Repulse* decommissioned in August 1996. The reins of the national deterrent, including a sub-strategic role, have now passed to the 'Vanguard' class SSBN, equipped with the Trident D5 missile – their story continues.

The power of splitting the atom! The potential of nuclear-powered submarines – the true submarine as opposed to existing 'submersibles' – freed from the handicap of charging batteries, ranging the oceans far and wide permanently submerged, limited only by the endurance of the crew, had been in the minds of submariners since the end of the Second World War. As early as 1948 Vice Admiral Sir 'Rufus' Mackenzie KCB, DSO*, DSC, a distinguished wartime CO and 'father' of the British Polaris Force, had submitted a paper to his Flag Officer Submarines which envisaged an underwater future along the lines of how air power had developed, with 'fighter' and 'bomber' submarines dominating the order of battle. It was the United States, with the commissioning of USS *Nautilus* in 1953, that first exploited this means of propulsion and developed the submarine from 'a platform of position' to a machine capable of relentlessly pursuing its targets.

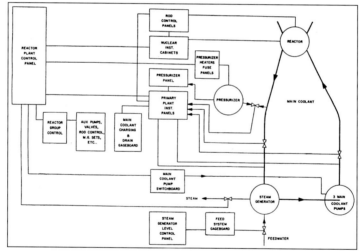

The basic layout of the pressurized-water reactor that drives nuclear-powered submarines. Pressurised primary loop water is driven through the reactor by main coolant pumps. In the reactor pressure vessel (RPV) it is heated to a very high temperature and flows into a steam generator (SG). Here it heats secondary water into steam, which rushes away to the main engines and electrical turbo-generators. The primary loop water, when it leaves the SG, is considerably cooler than when it entered so is driven back into the reactor to be heated up again. The greater the steam demand, the cooler (therefore denser) the primary water becomes, thereby slowing more neutrons available for the next phase of the fission process. Naturally the converse is true: less steam demand, the hotter the primary water is when it leaves the SG, fewer neutrons are slowed, therefore the lower the level of reactivity. The system is to a large degree, self-regulatory. The fission process is started by withdrawing control rods (made of a 'dull' element hafnium) from between the fuel plates.

The Atomic Energy Authority Experimental Research Establishment at Dounreay in Caithness, Scotland. It was here that all Royal Naval pressurized-water reactors were developed and tested before being produced by Rolls-Royce and Associates of Derby. All senior mechanical and electrical engineering staff involved with the propulsion side of the submarine received extensive training here at HMS *Vulcan*.

The Painted Hall at the Royal Naval College, Greenwich. It is difficult to imagine that in a building, less than two hundred yards from this astounding elegance, sat a 10 kilowatt training reactor called *Jason*. It was here at the Nuclear Power Training School within the college that all officers underwent their theoretical nuclear training. For seaman officers (including commanding officers) who simply needed to understand the basics, this was a course of a few months; for engineers who needed to understand their propulsion plants in great detail, the course was in excess of a year. One of the great strengths of the Royal Navy has been the principle of having specialists in each field of ship operation, and nowhere more than in the operation of our nuclear propelled submarines has this been better demonstrated.

Navy News

HMS *Dreadnought* passing the Rock of Gibraltar. The Royal Navy's first nuclear-propelled submarine was in fact half-American. In order to hasten the introduction of this highly powerful submarine into the RN Order of Battle, the United States provided the propulsion which was built by Westinghouse and supplied to Vickers Shipbuilders of Barrow who connected it to the British designed front end. To appreciate the joint US/UK enthusiasm to introduce the platform in the face of a growing Soviet threat, one only has to examine the UK's strategic proximity to the Norwegian and Mediterranean Seas – areas where it was essential for the West to exercise sea control.

Navy News

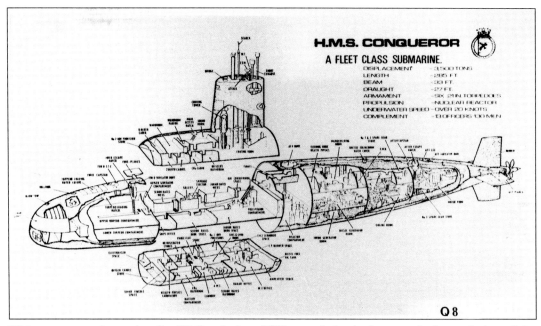

This cutaway schematic of a 'Valiant' class SSN reveals both the complexity and size of the machine. A capacious weapon stowage and sophisticated sensor suite plus the speed to travel quickly to any part of the world, underlines the superiority of the platform and the fundamental influence it was to have on future maritime warfare. In 1959 USS *Nautilus* triumphantly demonstrated the platform's immense capabilities by conducting a voyage under the Arctic ice to the North Pole. Similarly during a major NATO strategic exercise, *Nautilus* wreaked absolute havoc on the main striking forces of carriers, escorting vessels and attendant logistic vessels.

HMS *Dreadnought* arriving alongside at Singapore in 1967 after her epic non-stop, totally submerged voyage from the UK: a distance of 11,000 miles.

Captain Bob Garson

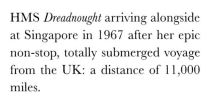

HMS *Valiant*, the first all-British-designed nuclear submarine entering the Clyde Submarine Base, Faslane, under typical skies. As well as providing many years of outstanding service under a number of distinguished commanding officers, she was to be the last survivor of the class (she paid-off finally in 1994) and served in the Falklands War under the command of Commander T. Le Marchand.

Navy News

HMS *Warspite* reflected in the mirror-calm water of the Gareloch and ready to come alongside at the Clyde Submarine Base. She and her sister 'Valiant' class SSNs were based in Scotland, and with two 'Oberon' class SSKs, made up the Third Submarine Squadron. These SSNs provided wonderful service during the height of the Cold War, mainly in surveillance and intelligence-gathering tasks against the ever-strengthening Soviet Navy. Those who served in them described them as the 'Queen of the Seas'.

HMS *Conqueror* in 1978, steaming ahead of a considerable flotilla with the flagship and helicopter cruiser HMS *Blake* in the centre, surrounded by her stores ships and escorts. This picture underlines one of the primary tasks of the SSN, namely protection of the fleet – indeed they are properly known as Fleet submarines. The SSN used its high speed and excellent sonar capability to operate well 'up threat' in the van of a Task Force in transit, countering any submarines or surface ships that threatened. On the Task Group's arrival in an operating area, the SSNs would take up defensive positions around it. It was this pattern of operations that was adopted by the four supporting SSNs during the Falklands War.

HMS *Conqueror* (Commander Chris Wreford-Brown DSO) with a bigger than usual casing party, entering the Gareloch after her epic patrol in the South Atlantic during 1982. Her Jolly Roger, the traditional flag flown by a Royal Navy submarine returning from a successful war patrol, can be clearly seen.

Navy News

A Mk VIII torpedo, the same type of weapon used by HMS *Conqueror* to sink the *Belgrano*, being loaded into HMS *Aurochs* in 1951. This is a particularly significant photograph since the officer loading the torpedo is Lieutenant Peter Herbert, who thirty years later and then a Vice Admiral, was Flag Officer Submarines during the Falklands conflict. The Mk VIII, although ancient in pedigree and unguided once it left the tube, was nevertheless a powerful torpedo with a range of 5,000 yd, delivering its 800 lb high explosive warhead at 45 m.p.h.

The teaching of torpedo attacks occurs during the Commanding Officers Qualifying Course, colloquially known as the 'Perisher' because of its traditionally high failure rate. Initial training is provided in a shore attack trainer, and the duty 'captain' can be seen at the periscope. Other prospective commanding officers in 1988 man stations in the attack team. Against the back wall is the torpedo calculator which passed angling information to the now-obsolete Mk VIII torpedo; the vertical plot is the Contact Evaluation Plot onto which all contact information from the submarine's sensors is transposed. The horizontal plot in the foreground is the Local Operations Plot which provided a fan of bearings and ranges from periscope observations from which the target course and speed could be deduced.

Navy News

Translation of the training into reality. Here a student's salvo of three practice Mk VIII torpedoes (set deep to run under the target) can be seen approaching a Type 21 frigate. The weapon runs a few yards ahead of the tell-tale track, so it looks as though he will have achieved one 'hit' at the stern, with a possible second success at the bow. The third weapon of the fan (achieved by angular spacing of the torpedoes) will almost certainly pass ahead. Firing these 'steam' weapons in salvoes was necessary to cover potential inaccuracies in the CO's fire control solution concerning the target's course, speed and range. Having the ability to 'guide' weapons towards the target, either visually or by sonar, eradicated to a large extent the need for costly salvoes.

A significant portion of the course is spent 'fighting' surface ships, which run to a set plan devised by 'teacher' to test the mental agility (and nerve) of the student CO to the full. Up to the mid-1980s a screen and target could consist of six ships, all buzzing around like high-speed bees. This frigate looks ominously close!

Commander Bob Mansergh

After a period of this type of running, frigates used to get blasé about the ease of detecting the 'target' submarine, so revenge had to be exacted in various ways. Note the submarine silhouette painted on the boot topping of the stern of HMS *Scylla*.

HMS *Courageous* 'on the step'. This was a configuration that could be achieved by the 'Valiants' when in the full-power state with maximum revolutions rung on. It meant, in simple terms, the submarine riding on its bow wave. One needed plenty of sea room to attempt it but it was good fun! On a more serious note, HMS *Courageous* was the first RN submarine to be fitted with the anti-ship Royal Navy Sub-Harpoon missile and, under the command of Commander Rupert Best, was another SSN deployed during the Falklands War.

Marconi Underwater Systems

The ship's magazine, produced every two weeks or so when on patrol, was a tremendous boost to morale and a great source of news and humour. It was unedited by the hierarchy and tended to be scurrilous, cutting, but never cruel. It also brought to the fore hitherto unrecognized talent with poets, cartoonists and comedians from the ship's company becoming regular, anonymous contributors. Perennially popular articles were 'Percy's Problem Page' – the submarine equivalent of the agony column – and the 'White Rat Corner' – overheard comments from the shop floor. The front cover of *The Thumper*, HMS *Churchill*'s magazine, was inspired by the captain's propensity for stamping his foot if things were not going to plan!

HMS *Churchill* on passage at sea. The submarine was named after Sir Winston Churchill, the first man to have had a Royal Navy ship named after him during his lifetime, and an honour felt proudly by all of her ship's companies throughout her life. It was fitting that his name should have passed to a submarine, since he always had great respect and affection for the crews who so gallantly gave their lives during the Second World War. Indeed, it was he who insisted that submarines should carry names rather than numbers, since he could not bear the anonymity bestowed on a man by being lost in a numbered submarine.

Every year there is a competition in the Submarine Flotilla for periscope photography. This shot by HMS *Spartan* showing HMS *Ocelot* being overflown by a Nimrod Patrol Aircraft was a prizewinner.

The 'Swiftsure' class SSN was introduced in 1973 to supplement the 'Valiant' class, and represented a steep change in capability over their graceful, yet rather old-fashioned sister submarines. They were faster, quieter and could dive much more deeply. The class consisted of HMS *Swiftsure*, *Spartan*, *Sovereign*, *Superb*, *Splendid* and *Sceptre*, and are now part of the First Submarine Squadron, based in Faslane. In 1994, the Third Submarine Squadron (SSNs and SSKs) amalgamated with the Tenth Submarine Squadron (SSBNs) to form the First, reviving its name after it was disbanded following HMS *Dolphin*'s demise as an operational base. This class were active during the height of the Cold War, and particularly distinguished themselves as intelligence gatherers.

HMS *Sceptre*, looking altogether more chunky, approaching the Clyde Submarine Base. Note the rudder hard over to starboard; 'S' class drivers would be the first to admit that these submarines were not the easiest to handle on the surface, particularly if you wanted to stop quickly. Underwater however, they were totally in their element. At full speed – in excess of 25 knots – and at maximum depth, it was possible to stand a pencil upright on the wardroom table without it wobbling!

HMS *Neptune*

HMS *Sovereign* approaching the Rhu narrows. The police boat escort is waiting to remain ahead of the submarine to ensure that no small boats get in her way in the relatively tricky navigation channel looming up. Note also the metric marking on her rudder. For old-fashioned submariners used to working in fathoms and feet, metres took some getting used to.

HMS *Neptune*

HMS *Superb* thundering down the Gareloch, with her escort 'nuclear tug' standing by to follow her. Like the police boat, the tug is another necessary escort in confined waters in case of a grounding or steering failure. Although tugs have very rarely been used in the thirty or so years of nuclear submarine operations at Faslane, their presence is reassuring, particularly in low visibility.

HMS *Neptune*

HMS *Splendid*, diving with both periscopes raised. SSNs are not built for quick diving, and the CO had to be careful to keep the propulsor underwater to avoid tripping his main engines. Once under, the submarine would be entirely in its own element, and could travel to any part of the world without hindrance, with food being the only limiting factor. HMS *Splendid*, under the command of Commander Roger Lane-Nott (later Flag Officer Submarines) gave valuable service during the Falklands War.

HMS *Spartan* passing Drake's Island on the way to her (then) home port of Devonport. The casing party is ranged far and wide, breaking out the berthing ropes stowed under the casing. She was another stalwart of the flotilla, and under the command of Commander Jim Taylor was the first SSN on station in the Falklands. It was fortunate for the task group that he made good time, because he was able to witness the Argentinians mining Port Stanley harbour.

Navy News

Good home base support is essential for successful and sustained operations. Because of limited onboard resources, the whole spectrum of support is required at a moment's notice: repair and maintenance facilities, comprehensive stores and weapon availability, comfortable, friendly rest and relaxation facilities, high-quality married quarters, pay and administrative support, technical and operational advice, and last but not least, pairs of welcoming arms after a tough patrol. This challenge has been consistently met by our bases, though they too have had their problems. For example, look at Faslane in the 1950s. All the facilities above are housed in the depot and repair ships, and submarines are scattered far and wide.

HMS *Neptune*

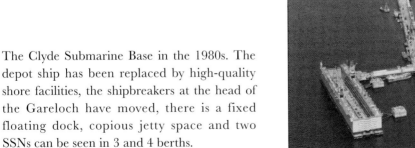

The Clyde Submarine Base in the 1980s. The depot ship has been replaced by high-quality shore facilities, the shipbreakers at the head of the Gareloch have moved, there is a fixed floating dock, copious jetty space and two SSNs can be seen in 3 and 4 berths.

HMS *Neptune*

The Clyde Submarine Base in the 1990s with the development of facilities for the mighty 'Vanguard' class SSBN complete. Of particular note is the ship lift facility at the northern end of the base. The magnificent countryside surrounding the Gareloch and Loch Long can be seen in its full glory.

HMS *Neptune*

The floating dock *AFD 60* in Faslane, with a 'Resolution' class SSBN securely on its blocks. The purpose of dry-docking is to allow access to the submarine's underwater fittings for examination and maintenance. Entry into the floating dock is achieved by the dock being flooded until only a few feet remain above the surface. The submarine is carefully driven to the entrance at which point wires, connected to powerful winches on the dock, are attached and it is hauled slowly into position above the blocks which will support it when it is dry and which have previously been positioned by the dock personnel. When the submarine is positioned within inches of accuracy, the dock then pumps water out of its huge internal flooding tanks and slowly emerges from the deep, bringing the submarine (now sitting on its blocks) up with it.

Navy News

The ship lift facility for the 'Vanguard' class in HM Naval Base Clyde, Faslane. To have built a floating dock capable of lifting this 18,000 ton monster would have meant it being the size of several football pitches! The alternative method of exposing the submarine's bottom, physically lifting it clear of the water on a cradle, was adopted and the machinery for achieving it is housed in the building pictured.

HMS *Neptune*

This unusual shot of HMS *Resolution* shows her conducting basin trials on completion of refit in Rosyth Dockyard in 1984. Although the Rosyth was the lead yard for Polaris submarine refits, it was also an important facility in sustaining the SSN refit programme. It is no longer used for such work.

Although there are no longer any operational submarine depot ships, limited support can be provided by deployed repair ships such as RFA *Diligence*, seen here with a 'T' class SSN alongside in the Falkland Islands.

The 'S' class was soon followed by the 'T' class, the first of which, HMS *Trafalgar*, was commissioned in 1983. Again, this class had taken advantage of every technological advance, most notably an improved reactor, and quickly established itself as an outstanding success. The class consists of HMS *Trafalgar*, *Torbay*, *Talent*, *Triumph*, *Trenchant*, *Turbulent* and *Tireless*. HMS *Trafalgar* is seen entering her home base of Devonport for the first time in September 1985. On the way she passes the aircraft carrier, HMS *Invincible* (note the Harrier aircraft astern), who had just suffered a hectic week of Navy Days.

Navy News

It is traditional, once every ten years, for those distinguished officers who have served as Flag Officer Submarines to gather for a reunion. Ranged in front of HMS *Andrew*'s 4 inch gun at HMS *Dolphin* in 1985 are, left to right, standing: Admirals 'Sandy' Woodward, Ewan Raikes, John Roxburgh, Ben Bryant, Tony Troup, 'Tubby' Squires, Dick Heaslip. Seated: Admirals 'Rufus' Mackenzie, Peter Herbert, Geoffrey Grantham, John Fieldhouse, Horace Law, 'Baldy' Hezlett, Ian McGeoch. These were the men, many of them Second World War heroes, who guided the submarine service through the technical revolution that witnessed the introduction of nuclear power and the Polaris Weapon System. Admiral of the Fleet, The Lord Fieldhouse (d. 1987) was the most senior submariner in history, and was Commander in Chief Fleet during the Falklands War, and later Chief of Defence Staff.

Navy News

HMS *Trenchant* on her commissioning day in January 1989. The picture of the ship's company arranged before their guests, and about to shoe-horn themselves into their boat, should dispel any myths about the amount of room available to the modern submariner!

Navy News

HMS *Turbulent* bow on, and looking very sinister. Note the absence of visible foreplanes on this class in comparison to the 'Valiants'. They were in fact below the waterline and only spread when the submarine was at slow speed and dived. Thus at speed and on the surface, they presented a highly hydrodynamic shape. The masts she has raised are wireless, with its extended high frequency section and the ultra high frequency 'christmas tree' at the top, and the search periscope with an electronic warning sensor above the upper visual window.

HMS *Neptune*

HMS *Triumph* conducting 'hands to bathe' in July 1991 during her sea trials. Note the swimmer of the watch dressed ready to leap in after anyone who gets into difficulty. In tropical climes there would be an armed sentry on the bridge as well to scare off any nosy sharks! This pastime was always very popular, especially with overheated engineers.

Navy News

HMS *Trenchant* looking rather the worse for wear after a long dived transit to Singapore. She has lost a number of her anechoic tiles designed to reduce her active sonar signature, but the problem looks worse than it actually is and could be fixed with glue and a lick of paint. More importantly, she had demonstrated the world-wide transit capability of the class.

HMS *Tireless* on the port bow leaving the Gareloch. The T boats form the Second Submarine Squadron in Devonport but are regular visitors to Faslane for such occasions as work-up and swift last minute checks should they be travelling further north. Note the outstandingly clean lines of this SSN.

HMS *Triumph* on her way into Faslane with the casing party enjoying the fresh Scottish air. A distinctive feature on the submarine from this angle is the towing hawser that runs down the starboard side of the fin. Should a highly unusual disaster befall the submarine and a tow be necessary, then the rope would be passed from the tug to the submarine, connected to the eye at the top of the bridge and then literally ripped out until the weight was taken by a permanently rigged towing slip in the bow under the casing.

Navy News

HMS *Torbay* being launched in March 1985 at Vickers Plc, Barrow in Furness. These submarines are capable of speeds in excess of 30 knots, depths in excess of 1,000 ft, are fitted with the latest sonar 2020, and armed with Spearfish torpedoes and Royal Navy Sub-Harpoon missiles.

Navy News

Rear Admiral Sir Anthony Miers VC KBE CB DSO* Commanding Officer of HMS *Torbay* during
the Second World War, attended the ceremony at Vickers Shipbuilders, Barrow. He is seen here
leaving the launch podium.

Navy News

HMS *Torbay* accompanying the SSKs of the Second Submarine Squadron, based in Devonport, in July 1987. Note the difference in sonar domes of the two conventional submarines.

Navy News

HMS *Triumph* entering Muscat, Oman with a dhow escort. The casing party are fallen in with officers in white socks and sailors in black. Her arrival in these waters re-emphasizes the world-wide capability of these vessels, as well as their ability to operate in a variety of climates.

Navy News

An American SSN at the North Pole, in total contrast to the sunshine of the Middle East. Note the thickness of ice penetrated, and the vertical configuration of the foreplanes. British and American designs for these planes were quite different in that the British placed them on the bow rather than the fin. Foreplanes are only really effective at relatively slow speeds (7 knots or so), with the majority of control being exercised by the after planes, sited adjacent to the propeller or propulsor.

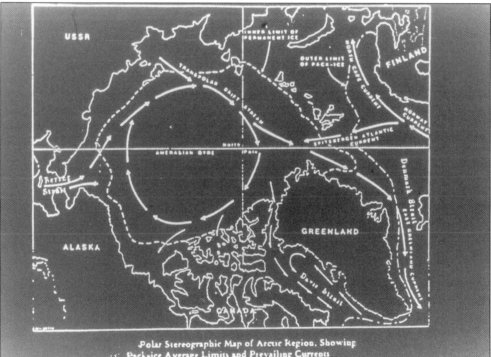

Polar Stereographic Map of Arctic Region, Showing Pack-ice Average Limits and Prevailing Currents

The explanation of the sensitivity of the Arctic ice pack. Control of this area provides instant access to the back door of the world's two superpowers and the ice canopy provides shelter for stooging Russian missile-firing submarines. It is essential for the West that their 'hunter-killers' have the capability to operate in these tricky conditions in order to find and prosecute their prey.

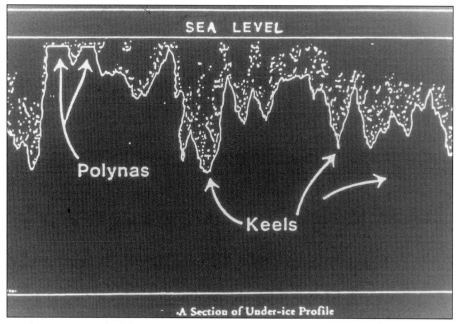

A cross-section of the ice canopy produced by an upward-looking echo-sounder. In summer there are polynas (areas of thin ice) that allow penetration of the ice-cap in order for submarines to surface for publicity shots.

HMS *Sovereign* at the North Pole in the dark of winter in 1976, with Commander Mike Harris (the CO) on the right, looking well wrapped-up against the cold.

Alternative uniforms for floodlit cricket at the North Pole. The teddy bear in the slips looks suitably alert.

Navy News

HMS *Superb* (left) and HMS *Turbulent* at the North Pole in 1987. Royal Navy submarines had previously visited the pole, but this was the first time that two had been there together. The coordination would have been achieved by the submarines talking to each other on underwater telephone, a useful device which is fitted in all Western ships and submarines and allows tactical communication with a submarine while it is deep.

Navy News

The picture taker. A Royal Air Force Nimrod Maritime Patrol Aircraft overflying HMS *Turbulent*. The Nimrod, a jet-driven MPA whose air-frame is based on the ill-fated Comet airliner, has been an outstanding success in a variety of surveillance roles, and there is close camaraderie between the Submarine Service and 'Coastal Command'.

A GEC-Marconi Tigerfish torpedo about to be transferred from a weapons lighter alongside an SSN in Faslane. The torpedo is wire-guided and remains connected to the firing submarine throughout its underwater flight towards the target. The command link conveys orders to the weapon to arm, steer left or right, alter its depth, and ultimately, when the torpedo gains contact on the target through its own sonar in its nose, provides permission to attack the target autonomously.

The Tigerfish on the loading rails of the submarine. It is heavily protected against scratching since its iodized skin provides essential protection against corrosion and maintains the weapon's fairness of form. The torpedo is locked into its belly-band and connected to the loading crane. As it is gently lowered by the crane, the wheels on the belly-band turn on the loading rails that lead down to the weapon stowage compartment: compare this picture to the one on p. 66, despite enormous changes in technology, there are some evolutions which remain the same.

The torpedo is disappearing through the torpedo loading hatch with its Tube Mounted Dispenser (TMD) attached. Wire guidance demands two separate elements of dispensing. There is the firing platform end (TMD) which accommodates the submarine's movement during the guidance phase, and there is the wire that is pre-loaded in the torpedo itself, and pays out during the weapon's flight.

The awesome damage inflicted on a target (ex-HMS *Lowestoft*) by the Tigerfish torpedo. The weapon has a combined direct (impact) fuse which would be most effective against other submarines, and a proximity (magnetic) fuse which would be the most likely effect triggered by a surface ship as the weapon passes a few feet underneath it. As can be seen, the resulting explosion creates a vortex in the water below the surface ship which leaves it unsupported in the middle, thereby breaking its back.

The firing sequence of the Royal Navy Sub-Harpoon anti-ship missile manufactured by McDonnell Douglas of the USA. In this first picture the nose cone of the capsule can be seen being blown clear. The missile has a range approaching 100 miles and thus can be fired from well outside the opposition's defensive ring, with minimal threat of counter-detection or attack against the SSN. At long ranges, selective targeting – absolutely guaranteeing a hit on the primary target – may not be possible so the SSN may be forced to a much closer range and to use torpedoes. However, the sea-skimming missile being small, fast and low, it is difficult to defend against it, even if detected early.

Targeting information (which direction to fly and when to switch on its homing radar) is passed to the weapon in the tube from the submarine's fire-control computer. The capsule is discharged when the captain has achieved his firing solution, and rises to the surface. A hydrostatic sensor in the capsule then triggers a small ordnance device which blows the nose-cap off, initiates the missile's booster motor, and it begins its flight towards the target.

The missile is boosted into a bunt where it stabilizes in flight and turns onto its pre-flight ordered course. It drops out of the bunt and then flies at a height that will provide it with sufficient time to adjust to its final approach course to the target, once its radar has detected it. The SSN CO will have determined the target range on firing as accurately as possible (bearing in mind that it is well over the horizon) so that the missile radar switch-on is as close to the target as possible, thereby providing minimum warning time for defensive measures to be initiated. Even then, the missile has several anti-countermeasure features that would ensure its success and heighten its effectiveness. The missile can be fired in salvoes to enhance the probability of defence penetration and damage enhancement. The earlier photographs show a weapon leaving a port tube; this one has been fired from starboard. Both capsules would have been given a left or right steer to avoid the submarine colliding with the sinking capsules.

Missile impact against the target. Although carrying a relatively small conventional warhead, it is delivered at such a speed and force that its residual fuel will immediately ignite and find its way quickly into the damaged area created by the missile's explosion.

The resultant damage to the hull of the target. It can be seen that the missile has in fact passed through the target and exited on the port side, but has left it crippled and totally out of action.

Since the introduction of the Royal Navy Sub-Harpoon missile, the adage has been adopted that missiles burn your enemy, and torpedoes sink him. The tangled mess on the upper deck is testimony to the havoc that would have been caused in between decks.

The Royal Navy needs no reminder of what a sea-skimming missile can achieve. This picture of HMS *Sheffield*, totally burnt out by the uncontrollable fire started by a French-manufactured Exocet missile which was fired by an Argentine Air Force Etendard aircraft during the Falklands War, tells the sobering story. It is worth noting that there is still doubt about whether the missile warhead exploded or not; the result shows that the discussion is irrelevant.

Two other capabilities of the SSN are depicted in the next two photographs. Special Forces can be seen dropping by parachute prior to being picked up by the SSN for onward transportation to their destination. It is a myth to assume that because the RN no longer has small diesel submarines that it has lost its 'cloak and dagger' role. Modern swimmer delivery vehicles that can be attached to the parent SSN have a significant range themselves, which in combination with the SSN's vastly improved speed, comfort, endurance and range over the SSK, means that a Special Forces team can be delivered to their objective anywhere in the world speedily, secretly and in excellent shape.

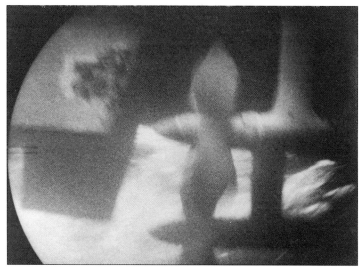

The underwater look, typical of the SSN's strength as an intelligence gatherer. While on the topic of comparisons between the SSK and its nuclear-powered counterpart, this is yet another area of classic submarine employment in roles of stealth and surprise in which the SSN excels. The SSK, no matter how many ingenious methods of propulsion are introduced, will always be a platform of position in that it relies, to a large extent, on its target coming to it. The SSN, because of its high speed and agility, is faster than any potential quarry and has the capability of being proactive in all its roles.

HM Queen Elizabeth, the Queen Mother, at HMS *Resolution*'s launch. Her Majesty was the ship's sponsor, and always maintained a close interest in the welfare of its ships' companies throughout its active service. The first Chief of the Polaris Executive, Vice Admiral Sir Hugh Mackenzie, observed in his autobiography *Sword of Damocles*, 'to ensure a submarine deterrent remained truly credible at all times, it required that, for week upon week when at sea, the crews were in all respects equivalent to being on patrol under conditions of war. Likewise to the submarines at sea on a schedule permitting not the slightest variation, required a similar approach from all those who worked ashore.'

Another major role of the SSN is the protection of its bigger sister, the SSBN. The 8,000 ton **HMS** *Resolution*, Britain's first ballistic missile carrying submarine, entering the water at Barrow after being launched on 15 September 1966. The Polaris programme was instituted in 1964 when the air-launched deterrent missile Skybolt, intended to be fitted to RAF V bombers, was cancelled by the United States on the grounds of cost and vulnerability. The Polaris system was provided instead under the Bermuda Agreement between President John Kennedy and Mr Harold Macmillan, the then Prime Minister. Although the missiles and their associated fire-control equipment were provided by the USA under the agreement, the warheads and their re-entry bodies were British designed and built to keep them under ultimate national control. Taking the deterrent underwater, keeping it mobile in undetectable platforms provided this weapon with a massive degree of security.

GOD GRANT THE WEAPON NEVER BE USED...

These words uttered by Vice Admiral Sir Hugh Mackenzie KCB DSO* DSC, a distinguished submarine commanding officer in the Second World War and the man charged with the introduction of the Polaris programme, echo the sentiments of the whole world. He was to oversee a programme of extraordinary complexity which required not only the building of four submarines of the highest quality, but also the production of all their equipment and the introduction of support facilities and training schools. He personally covered almost a quarter of a million miles in the air in keeping the project on track.

Vice Admiral Sir Hugh Mackenzie

The missile consisted of a two-stage, solid fuel rocket, whose differential steering motors sited at the base maintained the weapon on the target course, which was updated in flight and dictated by its integral guidance computer. It had a maximum range of 2,500 nautical miles, which allowed its parent submarine a great deal of flexibility in its choice of patrol area, away from the prying eyes and ears of the opposition. The missile was over 30 ft in length, 6 ft in diameter, and weighs close to 13 tons. The interstage and equipment sections contained the missile's integral computers which determine course adjustments, distance flown, and the moment that the payload should be released towards the target.

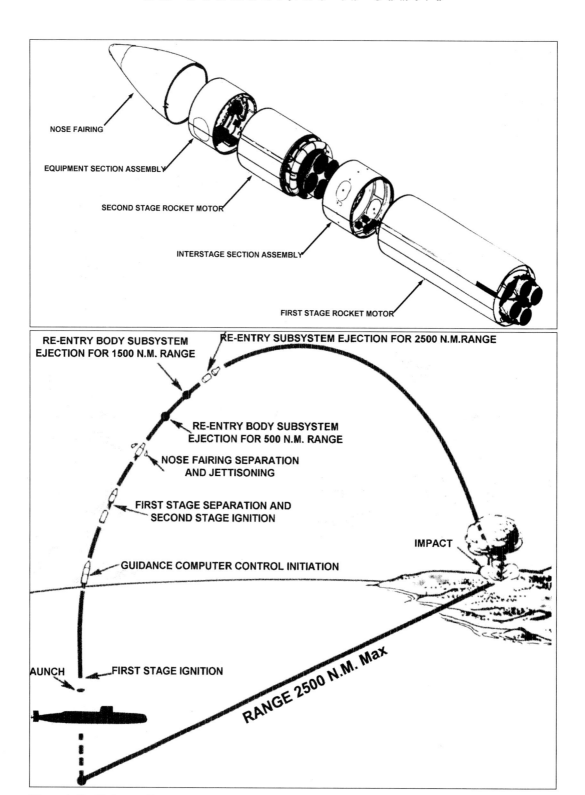

NOSE FAIRING

EQUIPMENT SECTION ASSEMBLY

SECOND STAGE ROCKET MOTOR

INTERSTAGE SECTION ASSEMBLY

FIRST STAGE ROCKET MOTOR

RE-ENTRY BODY SUBSYSTEM
EJECTION FOR 1500 N.M. RANGE

RE-ENTRY SUBSYSTEM EJECTION FOR 2500 N.M.RANGE

RE-ENTRY BODY SUBSYSTEM
EJECTION FOR 500 N.M. RANGE

NOSE FAIRING SEPARATION
AND JETTISONING

FIRST STAGE SEPARATION AND
SECOND STAGE IGNITION

GUIDANCE COMPUTER CONTROL INITIATION

IMPACT

LAUNCH   FIRST STAGE IGNITION

RANGE 2500 N.M. Max

The missile flight profile showing the principles of the ballistic delivery of its payload from space. The missile, when established in flight, rolls onto its required attitude and course for its target. The geographic position of the warheads' destination compared with the position of the firing submarine, dictate these settings and are determined by eleven different computers which contribute to the calculations. Navigational accuracy to within yards is therefore an essential capability for an SSBN, and is achieved by two Ships Inertial Naviation Systems (SINS) which sense the submarine's movement in every plane and apply the necessary updates to the navigation data bank.

Putting the deterrent into its historical context, with **HMS** *Resolution* being overflown by a Royal Air Force Shackleton Maritime Patrol Aircraft.

The Royal Navy Polaris School (with the tall tower) at the Clyde Submarine Base in Faslane. A mock-up of a Polaris missile is in the foreground, and the size of the missile can be judged against the car parked alongside it. The buildings behind the school make up the massive stores complex that supports the two submarine squadrons and parent establishment **HMS** *Neptune* that occupy the base.

A Sabot launch from an SSBN tube. This was a monster water slug driven out of the tube by the initiation of the gas/steam generator and was an essential precursor to a live missile launch. It can be seen that at its peak, the top of the slug is well above the height of the submarine's raised masts.

Navy News

The first Polaris launch in 1968 on the Atlantic Test Range off Port Canaveral, USA. This launch was achieved within the government's time scale and was a complete success. The speed at which the missile travelled into space and achieved the planned position for the delivery of its warheads into a ballistic trajectory towards its target made it extremely difficult to counter, thereby maintaining a fundamental requirement for a deterrent: guaranteed response in reaction to armed aggression. This, allied to the delivery platform's invulnerability, made the whole weapon system most effective.

Vice Admiral Mackenzie on the casing of HMS *Resolution* with Commander Ken Frewer, Commanding Officer of the Starboard Crew, and Captain Kenneth Vause, the Captain (S/M) Tenth Submarine Squadron. In order to maximize the use of the hulls, each submarine carried two crews known as Port and Starboard, with each crew conducting two patrols per year on roughly a three-month cycle. When the admiral was conducting initial briefings to the early crews, one wag commented that because of the cycle they would never be at home for the birth of their children. As quick as a flash the admiral responded 'Sorry about that, but I promise that I will have you there for the conception!'

Vice Admiral Sir Hugh Mackenzie

The Polaris missile soon after propulsion motor ignition. The 13 ton missile would have been lifted to the surface in a cloud of steam created by a gas/water generator sited at the base of the missile tube, and once clear of the sea surface, the first stage rocket motor ignites. Initiating keys for the gas generators are held by the commanding officer, and are only released on receipt of a properly authenticated firing signal. This is one of the checks and balances in the firing chain that prevents inadvertent or unauthorized discharge of a missile.

HMS *Resolution* on passage to Coulport, the missile preparation and storage base on Loch Long in Scotland. There were four such submarines built: HMS *Resolution* and *Repulse* by Vickers Shipbuilders in Barrow, and HMS *Renown* and *Revenge* by Cammell Laird Shipbuilders in Birkenhead. There was controversy when the fifth planned submarine was cancelled by the Labour government in 1967 because of contemporary doubts whether only four submarines could fulfil another essential facet of deterrence: constant vigilance and availability of response. In the event, the doubts proved to be unfounded and the decision justified, because when HMS *Repulse* conducted the last Polaris patrol in late 1996, the class had conducted 229 patrols in the twenty-eight years of their service, and the nation had enjoyed unbroken deterrent coverage. This was a remarkable achievement and a proud contribution to the peace of the world during periods of great political and military uncertainty.

Navy News

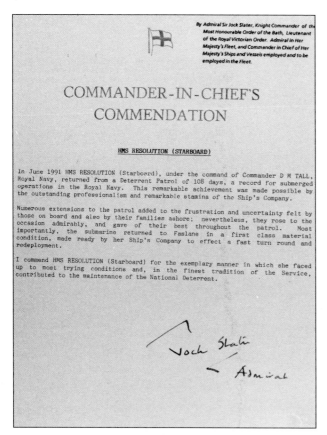

By Admiral Sir Jock Slater, Knight Commander of the Most Honourable Order of the Bath, Lieutenant of the Royal Victorian Order. Admiral in Her Majesty's Fleet, and Commander in Chief of Her Majesty's Ships and Vessels employed and to be employed in the Fleet.

COMMANDER-IN-CHIEF'S COMMENDATION

HMS RESOLUTION (STARBOARD)

In June 1991 HMS RESOLUTION (Starboard), under the command of Commander D M TALL, Royal Navy, returned from a Deterrent Patrol of 108 days, a record for submerged operations in the Royal Navy. This remarkable achievement was made possible by the outstanding professionalism and remarkable stamina of the Ship's Company.

Numerous extensions to the patrol added to the frustration and uncertainty felt by those on board and also by their families ashore; nevertheless, they rose to the occasion admirably, and gave of their best throughout the patrol. Most importantly, the submarine returned to Faslane in a first class material condition, made ready by her Ship's Company to effect a fast turn round and redeployment.

I commend HMS RESOLUTION (Starboard) for the exemplary manner in which she faced up to most trying conditions and, in the finest tradition of the Service, contributed to the maintenance of the National Deterrent.

Jock Slater
Admiral

The longest patrol by any Royal Navy submarine was achieved by the Starboard crew of HMS *Resolution* under the command of Commander David Tall in 1991. When these submarines went to sea they were effectively at war. The crews were totally on their own and entirely self-supporting while maintaining the three aims of the patrol: to remain undetected, to maintain constant communications and to be constantly ready to fire their missiles at short notice. Life at sea demanded the highest degree of teamwork and professional excellence from each member of the crew, particularly against the background of isolation from the outside world, apart from the daily newspaper transmitted from headquarters and occasional reception of the BBC's World Service. Families were able to send a 'familygram' to their loved ones, a forty-word message summarizing family news, every ten days.

The missile base at Coulport bathed in sunlight – a rare sight! It was at this base that the missiles were 'prepped' ready for loading. At the end of each patrol a number of missiles were offloaded for overhauling, the empty tubes used for training. After the retraining period at sea, following a joint crew maintenance session, the SSBN would berth alongside Coulport to replenish her load of 16 missiles.

RNAD Coulport

As part of the preparation to load a missile, a missile tube collar is fitted, seen here being loaded into position. The tube is 30 ft deep and is thus roped off for safety.

RNAD Coulport

The missile, inside its transport capsule, is being lifted by the loading crane for the next part of the loading sequence – marrying the capsule to the collar.

RNAD Coulport

Once this process is complete, the integral lowering gear in the capsule gently delivers the missile onto its flexible supports inside the submarine. This is an extremely delicate operation, conducted with the utmost care and precision.

RNAD Coulport

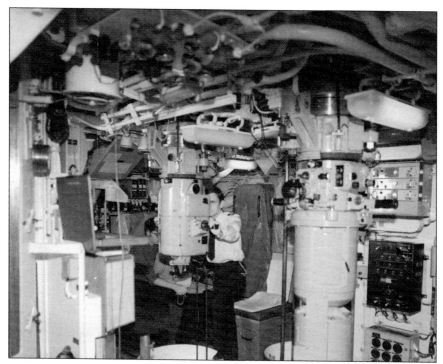

The control room of HMS *Revenge* during pre-sailing checks by the navigating officer who is checking the bearing accuracy of the attack (monocular) periscope; to his left is the raised search (binocular) periscope awaiting its turn. Once at sea this compartment would be full of bustle and activity as it became the submarine's nerve centre. The periscopes, incidentally, would be rarely used on patrol.

HMS *Repulse* leaving Coulport after finishing an outload and preparing for patrol. The casing party are conducting essential final checks on the bollard flaps that fold away when not in use. Anything that might slip or rattle on the casing was carefully insulated in order to avoid unwelcome noise interference once dived. The bandstand at the top of the fin was rigged during harbour operations to allow the captain to see both ends of his ship without risk of falling overboard!

HMS *Neptune*

The navigator checks the position of **HMS** *Renown* in the channel. Note the charts and bridge remote gyro repeat. Like the flagpole, this would be struck down below before diving; the 'holes' would be filled by hinged flaps as the final act of clearing the bridge for diving, thereby restoring the fin's fairness of form and minimizing 'flow' noise.

HMS *Neptune*

HMS *Revenge* on passage down the Clyde, soon to be in a position to start her patrol. She is doing 11 knots – note the wall of water she is pushing ahead of her. This passage to the diving position for patrol is always a period of great excitement and anticipation, tinged with the sadness of saying goodbye to loved ones. Getting to patrol on time with man and machine tuned to the highest standards was the driving ambition of everyone involved, and underpinned the enormous success of the Polaris programme.

The missile control centre during an exercise drill. The deputy Weapons Engineer Officer is holding the firing trigger that would initiate the firing sequence. This compartment contains the computers that pass targeting and positional information to individual missiles. The trigger itself is kept locked in a safe, whose combination is known only to the weapons engineer officer and his deputy, and is another check in the firing sequence. Note the emergency breathing mask around the neck of the standing junior rating. These would be broken out throughout the submarine during an emergency (e.g. in the event of a fire) or at 'action stations'.

HMS *Neptune*

The middle level of the missile compartment of an SSBN showing five of the sixteen missile tubes. The tubes, over 30 ft high and over 7 ft in diameter, are the hardware end of the operation and are extremely solid lumps of metal. This compartment was also known, for obvious reasons, as 'Sherwood Forest'.

Navy News

A personnel transfer to an SSBN being conducted by a Royal Navy Sea King helicopter at sea. The wind is in the perfect position of 15 degrees on the port bow to allow the pilot maximum visibility of his hovering reference mark. The personnel safety rail, into which belts would be clipped in rough seas for anyone on the casing, can be clearly seen meandering its way between the missile hatches on the after casing.

Navy News

HMS *Renown* on passage down the Clyde having just completed a course alteration.

HMS *Neptune*

Détente arrives. HMS *Revenge*, commanded by Commander David Morris, is visited by the Chief of General Staff, Soviet Armed Forces, General Vladimir Lobov (third from the left) at Faslane on 4 December 1991. Accompanying the Russian party is Vice Admiral Sir Hugo White, himself a submariner, and soon to become Commander in Chief Fleet. Astern of HMS *Revenge* is another SSBN, with an 'S' class SSN on 3 berth.

Navy News

The last word on Polaris, appropriately from **HMS** *Resolution* on her way to a final refit in Rosyth, to the permanent peace-campers parked on the verge of the roadway approaching the Clyde Submarine Base.

During the late 1980s the decision was made to replace the Polaris weapon system with the Trident D5 missile. This missile has a range of over 4,000 nautical miles and can carry twelve Multi Independent Re-entry Vehicles (MIRV), and first went to sea in the USN 'Ohio' class SSBNs. Four new RN submarines were required to carry sixteen of these monsters, and they are HMS *Vanguard*, *Victorious*, *Vigilant* and *Vengeance*.

HMS *Vanguard* is rolled out of the building hall at Vickers Shipbuilders in Barrow on 4 March 1992. This enormous submarine weighs in excess of 18,000 tons, is over 550 ft in length and 42 ft on the beam. She sports a revolutionary shaped design, and everything about her equipment represents a technological advancement. By mid-1996 she had already conducted two operational patrols, and her ship's companies have been delighted with her performance.

VSEL Link Newspaper

Another view of **HMS** *Vanguard* after roll-out, and this angle provides a breath-taking view of the submarine in all her enormity.

HMS *Neptune*

HMS *Vanguard* at sea. Her size is deceptive, and you have to look for the bridge watchkeepers to remind you of the height of the fin.

Some key compartments inside the 'Trident' class. The control room, with the remote sensing devices in machinery spaces and their computer-based displays. Admiral Sir Ben Bathurst, the First Sea Lord, visited HMS *Vanguard* in 1994.

HMS *Neptune*

The sound room with a significant bank of displays being fed from a myriad of sonar sets.

HMS *Neptune*

The Submarine Command System in the control room which receives information from the sound room. These banks of displays interpret the tactical picture, although it is interesting to see that old habits die hard and the Contact Evaluation Plot is still very much in evidence! The picture was probably taken when the submarine was on passage, which accounts for the paucity of contacts being plotted and the fact that SMCS is not being operated.

HMS *Neptune*

The Missile Control Compartment with WEO holding the training fire trigger.

HMS *Neptune*

The ship control position in **HMS** *Repulse* with a supply department bonanza! The petty officer cook stands between the petty officer stores accountant on the after planes, and the leading writer on the foreplanes.

HMS *Neptune*

The lone sentry on the casing of HMS *Vanguard* alongside in Cape Canaveral.

HMS *Neptune*

The proud officers of HMS *Victorious*, the second 'Trident' to be commissioned. Commander Huntley Gordon (centre) is accompanied by a number of his officers.

HMS *Neptune*

HMS *Vigilant* on the blocks, with the final 'Trident' class, HMS *Vengeance*, inside the building hall at an early stage of construction.

HMS *Neptune*

This wonderful picture of HMS *Vigilant* at night taken by Vickers Plc, proves beyond doubt that the submarine and her weapon system has teeth!

VSEL Link newspaper

A final piece of nostalgia. In 1993 the Royal Navy said goodbye to three of its submarine classes; two had been outstanding servants, and the third had promised so much: HMS *Valiant*, HMS *Olympus* and HMS *Upholder*.

INDEX